CW00740065

THE RED ROSES

THE RED ROSES

*Behind the Scenes with the
England Women's Rugby Team*

Jessica Hayden

First published in 2024 by
Arena Sport, an imprint of
Birlinn Limited
West Newington House
10 Newington Road
Edinburgh
EH9 1QS
www.arenasportbooks.co.uk

Copyright © Jessica Hayden 2024

The right of Jessica Hayden to be identified as the Author of this work has been
asserted by her in accordance with the Copyright, Designs and Patents Act 1988.

All rights reserved. No part of this publication may be reproduced, stored or
transmitted in any form without the express written permission of the publisher.

ISBN 978 1 91375 916 2

British Library Cataloguing-in-Publication Data
A catalogue record for this book is available from the British Library

Typeset by Initial Typesetting Services, Edinburgh

Papers used by Birlinn are from well-managed forests and other responsible sources

Printed and bound by Clays Ltd, Elcograf S.p.A.

This book is dedicated to every Red Rose, former and present, who put their bodies on the line for their country and led the way for today's crop of Red Roses. It's also dedicated to the female organisers and administrators who faced mammoth challenges and opposition in the early days of international women's rugby and did it anyway.

When women work together, we achieve incredible things. Thank you.

CONTENTS

ACKNOWLEDGEMENTS

I had no introduction to rugby until I went to Swansea University, where I studied politics. I wanted to join the football team and went to the freshers' fair with my heart set on being a central midfielder. The football coach was on his phone and didn't stop texting to answer my questions about joining. Feeling quite downtrodden, I carried on wandering around the fair and saw a girl with a can of cider in her hand, pouring it all over her face. She was doing a straight-arm pint, or something like that. She had to try and drink her cider without bending her elbow. I could see her bruised legs and could hear her team-mates clapping her on. Whatever club she was in, I wanted to join. I walked over and introduced myself and she gave me a sip of her cider. She told me her name was Clara and she played rugby for the university. I signed up instantly.

I went along to my first training session and there was Siwan Lillicrap, who later went on to become the Wales captain. At the time she was the director of rugby at Swansea University and my first impression of her was that she was bloody scary. Her thick Swansea accent was made harder to understand because she seemed to shout everything. I was relieved when another coach said, 'You're with me, mush.' The coach was Sam Cook, or Cookie, as I knew him. I had turned up in a South Africa rugby jersey which had been a birthday present (only because I was in South Africa for my birthday, not because of any real interest in rugby), and Cookie had seen that and assumed I was therefore a rugby player. He demonstrated a gentle tackle on me, walking through the stages of placing cheek to bum cheek, wrapping arms and putting the player on the floor. I remember thinking I needed to keep a strong face and pretend it didn't hurt. At the end of the session, Cookie asked me if I would like to play in the 'Old Girls' fixture on the Wednesday, two days on from that first training session. Like any good fresher keen to look a lot braver than they really are, I said yes, unaware that I had just signed up to play a full-contact rugby match against players including Siwan. Off to Sports Direct I went, ready to spend as little of my student loan as possible on a pair of rugby boots and a gum shield.

I didn't make a single tackle or pass the ball once. Well, that stretches the truth a bit. There was one pass I made, but it's not a story I'm too proud of. Someone, for some unknown reason, passed *me* the ball and running towards me came Siwan. In that split second I had three choices: try and take this ball into contact (with no idea about how to present the ball), turn back and run away from Siwan, or stand still and piss my pants. In the end I just handed the ball to Siwan so she wouldn't tackle me. My rugby skills have improved only marginally since then.

As the years progressed, I made some wonderful friends who are the most fun people in my life. Clara turned out to be the best influence on me because she dragged me out of my shell and forced me to face my fears all the time. She made me braver and more able to stand up for myself. I also met two of my closest friends, Monique Latty and Angelika Jankowska, thanks to our days playing rugby at Swansea Uni. Joining rugby often made me behave terribly, broke my bones and gave me the ability to funnel a pint in under ten seconds. But most importantly, it gave me the most incredible friends. I go to rugby matches and bump into girls I used to play rugby with, I present events and spot faces in the crowd whom I once shared a huddle with. Women's rugby is a community of women who will challenge you, get the best out of you and party with you afterwards. When women work together, we achieve incredible things. There is no group or setting I have been in that is quite like those days of playing university women's rugby.

It gave me other things too, not least of which is my partner Nick, who coached women's rugby at Swansea University. He would probably sue me if I don't mention that he never coached me, but he was one of the coaches (don't blame me for dating one of the coaches, I watched *Bend It Like Beckham* growing up . . .). Anything tactical about rugby in this book, or anything I write, tends to be sense-checked by him. He was the first man I knew who was truly committed to women's rugby. He coached the Swansea Women (known as 'The Whites'), who were the best Premiership team in Wales for years, and self-funded his trip to the 2017 Women's Rugby World Cup to support the players out there whom he coached at club level. People often say how lucky I am to have a partner who understands my world so well, but he was in this world long before me. And really, I had to pick someone who loved women's rugby or else I would have nothing to talk about. Women's rugby really is my entire personality.

But the most important thing that rugby gave me in those early days was my career. I studied politics at Swansea and tried to write every essay about feminism. I love learning about women's rights, and to this day whenever I type 'women's rugby' on my phone, autocorrect asks me if I mean 'women's rights'. Can you sense yet, reader, how utterly obsessed I am with women misbehaving? For me, women's rugby was a gateway into a world of women who were pushing against the status quo, working really hard, and frankly, looked like me. In my third year, now friends with Siwan and no longer completely terrified, I had a conversation with her about her week. She had a full-time job as director of rugby at Swansea University, but also played for Swansea Whites, Ospreys and Wales. Every single day of her week, from the early morning to the late evening, was spent either coaching or playing rugby. She was remarkable. It made me wonder if rugby fans realised the sacrifices women make to play international rugby.

I knew I wanted to be a journalist and had sort of expected to go into political journalism when I graduated. I had no contacts in the field but I had been writing for political blogs since I was 15, under a male alias, and had even been in a Channel 4 documentary about my feminist activism. By the time I was at university I had been invited to the House of Commons to speak about sexism in the media and how it affected young girls. At age 16 I had been on ITV's *This Morning* to speak about wanting to get rid of page three (for those unfamiliar, some national newspapers used to have boobs where there should be news on page three). I had no fear of speaking out and when Siwan told me about her week, I felt like my love for rugby could be used to do good, and I started a plan to become a women's rugby journalist.

I applied for work experience at *The Times* and feigned interest for a week at *The Sunday Times Magazine* while slowly walking past the sports desk every day until I eventually mustered up the courage to introduce myself. I secured a week of work experience there, during the Six Nations. In that week, a male journalist at the paper had written a piece suggesting that the Women's Six Nations should be moved to Wednesday nights so that the matches didn't clash with the men's Six Nations and therefore more fans watched. Did he not realise they had jobs? I pitched an idea to write about the sacrifices international women's rugby players make, spoke to players from Wales and Ireland – including Doctor Claire Molloy who played for Ireland at the time – and in the paper it went. The sports desk was impressed and asked me to stay on for another week. I wrote even more, and it was the start of my career, which now sees me write about women's rugby, present matches and talk about it on the radio and TV. For me, it is the greatest job in the world.

Writing this book has been a labour of the purest love. I adore women's rugby. I love the players, the people and the stories. Women's rugby is so much a part of me that I'm not sure if there's much else left. Thank you for supporting me, by buying this book, and letting me write so much about it.

I want to say thank you to everyone who spoke to me for this book, both on the record and off, with particular thanks to Marlie Packer, Jess Breach, Emily Scarratt, Maud Muir and Abbie Ward for their support.

And last but certainly not least: a heartfelt thank you to my family and friends. Writing a book is incredibly selfish. I have lost count of the plans I have had to cancel in order to write this book while working full-time for *The Times*. It has been an incredibly busy time. My partner Nick has been a great support, as have my parents Tracy and Neil, my twin brother Mark, my two remaining grandparents: Nana Chris and Nanny Pam, and my extended family, with special mention to my uncle Gareth, who have all bravely asked, 'How's the book going?', and even more bravely, stuck around for the answer.

I would like to finish with a final acknowledgement to my Grandad Den, whose portrait sits proudly on my desk as I type this sentence, and as I have typed this entire book. In the photo his tie is skew-whiff, he has my mum's red sun hat on, and he has a cigarette balancing between his lips. It was taken after a particularly good night out, I am told. He was the most incredibly funny man, whom I loved and cared for deeply. He really didn't like women's rugby, or more specifically, he really didn't like *me* playing women's rugby, but he kept a collection of my published work next to him in his chair and I know he would have been so proud of me for writing this book.

INTRODUCTION

The bitter taste of an unattained pinnacle hung in the air as the England women's rugby team stood still, hands on hips, taking in deep breaths of cool air in Eden Park stadium. They could barely move, almost frozen in time, as they watched New Zealand celebrate wildly only metres away from the try line where the Red Roses had gathered, crestfallen. The New Zealand crowd roared, lights flashed, and the sound system blared out celebratory music, but for the England team, there was only silence.

The Red Roses watched the world move on without them. Every minute felt like an hour as the players' eyes stung and their lungs burned with anguish for the game just lost, slowly processing what had just happened. Their bodies were worn out from a long tournament and their hearts were shattered. The weight of expectation and the relentless pursuit of glory converged into a single devastating moment of realisation. They had lost the World Cup final, again. It was a reminder that in the arena of sport, victory and defeat are inextricably entwined, each lending meaning to the other, juxtaposed in the close quarters of a rugby pitch as one team dances and the other cries.

Each player's mind was filled with questions of what ifs and what abouts. The match had been lost in one single moment that would define so much that followed. With the clock ticking close to full-time and the Red Roses behind 34–31, hope ignited in the eyes of the England players as they were given the penalty that could save them. The decision was made to kick the ball straight out, from the five-metre line, and aim for a last-gasp try, a kick to the corner, a lineout and a driving maul; the cornerstone of England's game. The tension reached its climax as the ball sailed towards the corner, and as the Red Roses rushed into their positions, they knew that everything was riding on this one act. Years of practice, hours upon hours of perfecting this move – which even had its own name, the 'Tank' – came down to one final moment. The steadfast dedication and unspoken sacrifices hung above each player's head as they arrived to their position.

The ball was thrown and destiny hung on a precipice, suspended between triumph and heartbreak. If the ball lands in England's hands, they can win the World Cup. If it falls to New Zealand, England lose the World Cup. Amidst the chaos of bodies grappling in the air, fate wrote its next chapter. With a ruthless display of skill and timing, New Zealand seized the opportunity that presented itself. In a fleeting moment of anguish, the ball slipped from the grasp of Abbie Ward, the England forward, into the clutches of the Black Ferns.

England were on a 30-match winning streak before this game. 'Sport is cruel,' uttered Sarah Hunter, the England captain in the final, moments after the final whistle had blown. She had been here before. New Zealand are England's closest rivals and had beaten them in four World Cup finals before this one. Sarah had played in two of them, now three.

As the team moved slowly together and ambled into the changing rooms, words were quietly spoken and friends were embraced, in shock at what had just unfolded. For many of the players, this was the first time they had lost in an England shirt.

The journey from crestfallen warriors to resilient champions begins anew, immediately. It is in these moments of profound disappointment that the true character of a team emerges. In the days, weeks and months that followed, the team gathered their shattered dreams and channelled their resilience into determination. Never would they feel that way again. The pain of loss cuts deep. Never again.

And so, with a heavy heart but a strong resolve, they gather the fragments of their hopes and set their sights on the future, knowing that defeat today may well fuel the fire of triumph tomorrow.

Their challenge now is working out how to turn winners into champions. The team know how to win, but why couldn't they win on the biggest stage? And what, if anything, can be gleaned from a match where victory hinged on the slightest of margins? It was in that very pursuit that the team turned to the percentages. As they regather and rebuild, they look at the 1 per cent improvements they could each make to take them that one, crucial, step further.

As a rugby journalist with a front-row seat to the captivating story of the Red Roses, I have witnessed first-hand the dedication, passion and resilience that define this remarkable team. I've followed their highs and reported on their lows, always inspired by their spirit. This is a special team full of exceptional women: they were the girls who insisted on playing with the boys, the teenagers who defied negative comments about women's rugby, and are now the women who put their bodies on the line for the game they love.

I felt compelled to share their tale, offering you an intimate glimpse into the inner workings of one of the most revered rugby teams in the world. From the warmth of their homes to the hallowed grounds of training camps, players, coaches and staff (former and present) have graciously welcomed me into their fold. The team's management have allowed me into the training camps and in meetings that are usually closed to the outside world, and the Red Roses have shared previously untold stories about life as elite women rugby players.

But why now, you might ask? In recent years, as interest in women's rugby has developed, a growing fan base has emerged, hungry for a deeper understanding of the players they adore. An ITV documentary called *Wear the Rose* – which aired in November 2022 to preview the 2021 Rugby World Cup, ultimately played in 2022 due to the unforeseen circumstances of the coronavirus pandemic – showcased the players and staff who help the team go to new levels. As a rugby consultant on that project, I had the privilege of working closely with the production team, providing insights into the squad's characters and illuminating the key storylines to follow in the lead-up to the tournament. This book, in many ways, serves as an extended cut of that documentary, presenting you, the reader, with an exclusive invitation to venture behind the scenes, to unravel the intricacies of the squad like never before.

Together, we will unveil the untold tales, the hidden struggles and the indomitable spirit that define this powerful collective.

'A book about the Red Roses?' Marlie Packer, the England captain, asked, on a phone call just a couple of months after those World Cup exertions. 'Will I be in it?'

'Yes, you'll be in it,' I replied. 'That's why I'm calling you.'

'I guess I'll have to read it then,' she said. 'What are you going to say about me?'

The narrative begins by delving into the very origins of the Red Roses, tracing the humble beginnings of women's rugby in England. It pays homage to the pioneers and trailblazers who have laid the foundation for the team's ascent. To truly grasp the awe-inspiring nature of the current squad, we must take a moment to reflect on their historical context and remember the genesis of the game. From grassroots movements to the advent of professional contracts, and from horrified men stopping matches to world-record crowds, we'll explore the pivotal moments that have moulded this team into the powerhouse they are today.

At the heart of this tale is the current squad, a remarkable group of athletes who have captivated the rugby world's attention with their phenomenal skill and character. A modern history of the team shines new light on the rocky road from the amateur era to professionalism. The traits needed to become a Red Rose are also explored as four players from different backgrounds are followed on their quest to play for England. We'll delve into their stories, the personal moments of triumph and their setbacks, to better understand the pressure on the shoulders of the England team.

The search by players and staff for the 1 per cent advantage they hope will win them the World Cup in 2025 is also examined and the background work that makes the Red Roses so successful is revealed, considering all elements of the high-performance environment that have propelled them to the pinnacle of sport. Conversations with unsung heroes, from the team's nutritionist to the analyst, and every backroom staff member in between, offer insight into the hard-working men and women whose work often goes without mention. Crucially the culture in the squad, including where it has gone wrong in the past, and what needs to change in the future, is also put into sharp focus.

A deep dive into the on-pitch rugby, not only unravelling the tactical revolution that spurred England to a 30-match winning streak, but also considering (with help from a number of coaches and coach educators) how coaching women's rugby is so different to the men's game, concludes with a thought to how England's tactics on the pitch have changed the game forever. But is that enough when they don't win the World Cup?

Every aspect of the team's World Cup journey in the 2021 tournament is also scrutinised. From the heartbreaking tales of non-selection to the previously untold stories of camaraderie behind the scenes, this book is there for every moment of an unforgettable competition.

The path ahead for the Red Roses is, naturally, the most pressing topic. In the aftermath of the 2021 World Cup the team went through a period of mass change, on and off the pitch, as coaches and captains left and attendance records were broken. The team is now on its way to greater heights but the road ahead has the potential to deliver more dramatic chapters in a captivating story.

Importantly, the off-pitch issues that lie in England's path to success are also studied. From rugby's battle with concussion, maternity right negotiations and social media abuse, the obstacles England – and women's rugby in general – face are significant.

Beyond the glittering accolades and devastating losses, our exploration will extend to the broader impact of the success of the Red Roses. Their rise to prominence has not only enthralled audiences but has also ignited a fervour for women's rugby, inspiring a new generation of players and fans alike. We'll examine how their performances have led to increased participation figures and heightened recognition for women's rugby in England and beyond, forever shaping the landscape of the sport.

The 2025 Rugby World Cup is on England's home turf. It is important to look ahead to that tournament, contemplating its significance and its potential to elevate women's rugby in England to new heights. We'll consider the impact of England's women's football team winning the women's European Championships, and if the Red Roses could grip the nation like the Lionesses did in 2022.

In writing this book, my sense of the team has been transformed, my respect deepened and my interest piqued. The Red Roses are a resolute group of remarkable women whose collective spirit radiates a brilliance that transcends sport. They are not just rugby players; they are role models, inspirations, feminist icons. But they won't tell you that, so I will. These extraordinary and powerful women, driven by a hunger for success, exemplify courage and bravery not only in sport but in their entire lives. They have a rare calibre that would guarantee success in whatever field they turned their hands to and yet they chose rugby union, and for that, we are eternally grateful.

Chapter 1

THE PIONEERS

Women's rugby is a feminist issue. It always has been. Rugby is traditionally a male sport, and for many years it was seen as too violent for women. Being a rugby player goes against the gender stereotype of womanhood; it's messy, brutal, loud, confrontational and dirty. And it's wonderful. The appeal of the sport goes beyond a means of protest, of course, but its heart is in challenging the standards set by men and its history is in pioneers who have never taken a step back on their fight for the sport.

To play rugby as a woman has often been considered in history as a political statement; a chance to visibly show what women's bodies were capable of. And for over a century, women's rugby was vastly unpopular. So unpopular, in fact, that during the first women's rugby match on record in England, spectators ran on to the field to stop play. A newspaper report from the time read: 'The lady footballers played on the old Southcoates ground opposite the Elephant and Castle, Holderness Road, on Good Friday, April 8th, 1887. The spectators broke into the playing area and stopped the match.'

It is within the context of such adversity that the spirit

of women's rugby was born. The significance of the sport reaches far beyond the touchlines of the playing field; it embodies a fight for recognition, a quest for equality, and a belief in the power of women's resilience.

Dr Victoria Dawson, a historian exploring female involvement in rugby league, discovered evidence of this first women's rugby match on English soil while trying to work out who the first woman or girl documented as playing rugby in the world is. Also in 1887, a ten-year-old girl called Emily Valentine joined in with her brothers when their school team, in Ireland, was a player short. Emily is often credited with being the first girl to play rugby, thanks to John Birch from Scrum Queens who discovered her diary, but of course it's likely there were other girls who played the sport with brothers in gardens or behind closed doors. But it was never documented, because such an act would be seen as inappropriate and unwomanly.

In sharp contrast to the disdain of early women's rugby reports in the British media, New Zealand seemed to be far more supportive of their women's rugby players. In 1891, a newspaper report spoke positively about the sport and detailed the support around the players. The 'enterprising young damsels', as the newspaper article uncovered by Professor Jennifer Curtin reads, had their hair cut short to 'prevent accidents' and would be 'provided with costumes designed so as to give the freest use of their limbs, consistent with their ideas of propriety'. The text reads as far more supportive of the women, suggesting they have 'a fair degree of proficiency in manipulating the leather'.

Across the world in the late 19th century, women were beginning to challenge their gender roles and campaigns for the right to vote gathered steam. In New Zealand, women's rights movements had comparatively good support and it was the first country to grant women the right to vote in 1893.

In Britain, the Victorian era held strong beliefs about ideals of femininity and masculinity. Women were expected to limit their ambitions to marriage, motherhood and having a clean house. Those beliefs were ingrained in the fibres of society and generally followed, despite Queen Victoria being a powerful monarch. 'The woman's power is for rule, not for battle,' wrote imminent social thinker John Ruskin in 1865. 'And her intellect is not for invention or creation, but for sweet ordering, arrangement, and decision ... she must be enduringly, incorruptibly good; instinctively, infallibly wise, wise not for self-development, but for self-renunciation: wise, not that she may set herself above her husband, but that she may never fail from his side.' So not much time for rugby training, then.

It would take the First World War to shift attitudes towards women. With men away at the front, many women took up jobs that had previously been seen as too dangerous for women. They operated dangerous machinery, sometimes were exposed to harsh chemicals, and often had to transport heavy goods like coal. The idea of women's work completely changed during this time.

One role that a lot of women turned to was keeping the munitions supply chain roaring along during the war. The women who worked in those factories became known as 'munitionettes' and factory owners often allowed their workers to form sports teams in a bid to boost morale and keep the workforce fit. In a time when attitudes were

shifting and women were finding their power, some munitionettes chose to play rugby.

By 1918, the year the First World War ended, there was
a well-received and popular women's rugby set-up in Wales,
particularly on the industrial south coast, as Dr Lydia Furse,
a women's rugby researcher, found. On 29 September 1917,
there was a women's rugby match at the Cardiff Arms Park
between two teams from the Newport munitions factory,
which was described by the *Western Mail* at the time as
'a wonderful display of scrimmaging, running, passing,
and kicking' and said the players 'pleased the spectators
immensely by their vimful and earnest methods.'

The movement peaked when 10,000 people were reported
to have attended a match between Cardiff and Newport on
15 December 1917 at the Cardiff Arms Park. Maria Eley,
the full back for Cardiff, remembered the match 83 years
later, the year before she died: 'It was such fun with all of
us together on the pitch, but we had to stop when the men
came back from the war, which was a shame. Such great fun
we had.'

At the same time as rugby's much smaller revolution,
England's flourishing women's football scene was gaining
international acclaim. Its roots were also in the munitions factories that women had kept going while the men
were away with the war. Many war factories across the
UK had a women's football team. In Preston, women at
the Dick, Kerr & Co factory formed a football team and
trained around their shifts. As their skills developed, they
challenged a neighbouring factory, the Arundel Coulthard
Foundry, to a competitive game to raise money for charity.
They drew in a crowd of 10,000 people who watched the

Dick, Kerr Ladies win 4–0. 'Dick, Kerr's were not long in showing that they suffered less than their opponents from stage fright, and they had a better all-round understanding of the game,' read a report in the *Daily Post* at the time. 'Their forward work, indeed, was often surprisingly good, one or two of the ladies showing quite admirable ball control.'

Across the country, women's football was soaring in popularity. The matches were known to attract 50,000 spectators and the proceeds were often donated to support injured servicemen. Alas, men returned from war and for most women, life soon reverted back to how it had been before. Some, not all, women were granted the vote in 1918, but the efforts of women to emancipate themselves in other areas of life had largely fallen flat.

Women's football gathered steam for another few years, and in 1921 the Dick, Kerr Ladies reached a new height. They played over 60 games of football that year, on top of full-time jobs, in front of an estimated total of 900,000 fans. The roaring success of the sport faced an abrupt end on 5 December 1921, when the Football Association (FA) issued a ban which did not allow any member club to let women's teams play on their grounds. The FA were worried that the popularity of the women's game would take money away from the men's game after the war, and also suggested the money raised from women's football was being spent 'frivolously' when they believed more of the money should have gone to charity. No such rule existed in men's football.

Women's football was sidelined. Minutes from the meeting called football 'quite unsuitable for females' and decided it 'ought not to be encouraged'. Leading doctors began to agree that football was unsuitable for women. They said the physical nature of the sport was too much for women to handle and could prevent women becoming pregnant. Women had proved their physical abilities in the war but had been once again been tied down to the roles society at the time handed to them: stay home, have children and be a good wife.

Women's rugby in the United Kingdom did not recover after the war and the efforts of those early pioneers were largely forgotten in history. It wasn't until the 1970s, amid the second wave of feminism, that women's rugby took off once again. This time it was universities who introduced women to the sport; firstly in the USA, Canada and France. Interestingly, there is evidence in France of a version of rugby deemed more suitable for women, called *barette*, being developed in the 1920s. In the USA, women's rugby proved vastly popular, which some believe is because rugby union was not a popular sport for men, and therefore women received less opposition to playing it. Kevin O'Brien, the head coach of the USA team who won the inaugural Women's Rugby World Cup in 1991, says rugby had become a political statement for American women. 'A lot of the women involved weren't supposed to be doing this, but basically they said, "Screw you, you can't stop us; we're going to play," because there was a lot of resentment and a lot of putting down of women in sport,' he told me in 2022. 'It was on the forefront, the cutting edge of women in sport. Well, there were no other contact sports. The rules in this country [the USA] for all sports are different for women. So for a lot of women, to get out there and play in a contact sport was a political statement.'

It is no coincidence that rugby attracts women during the waves of feminism. It is one of the most physically challenging sports for women. People of all shapes and sizes can thrive in rugby – no longer constricted to being small – and the sport teaches assertiveness and aggression in a way that society for so long deemed inappropriate for women. Across the world, playing rugby was a way of repealing the constructs of society and physically asserting their abilities.

In England, women's rugby hubs began to appear around the country with students and graduates, with many teams who would gather at an annual tournament in Loughborough. In February 1982, University College London (UCL) travelled to France to play teams including Pontoise, and found a well-organised domestic competition there that ignited a desire to lift the game in Great Britain. As such, the idea of the Women's Rugby Football Union (WRFU) was founded.

The union represented players from England, Wales and Scotland with 12 founding teams, all from universities in England, except the Magor Maidens, a rugby club in South Wales. The organising committee planned a meeting at the Bloomsbury Theatre in Euston in 1983 to discuss their objectives, and at first decided to focus on growing the participation of women's rugby and establishing teams outside of universities. But when a touring team from America, known as the Wiverns, came to visit and won 44–0 on two separate occasions, it prompted the realisation from the WRFU that the creation of a Test side was a crucial next step for the union, to limit the risk of Great Britain being left behind as countries such as the US, France and the Netherlands led the way with strong women's rugby teams.

Great Britain played a total of eight matches in the following years, but by the mid-eighties each respective country felt strong enough to begin to establish their own national teams. In 1987 England played Wales, winning 22–4 at Pontypool Park.

The next four years were monumental for the development of women's rugby globally. National teams were forming and competing, leading to the idea that there really should be a World Cup for the women. But the International Rugby Board (IRB), which is now World Rugby, had little interest in supporting such an idea, and the women's game in England was still operated solely by volunteer administrators and, frankly, hard-working women who refused to take no for an answer.

When Richmond, a hub of women's rugby in south London, toured New Zealand in 1989, they shared contact details with the teams in Canterbury and Christchurch with the idea of playing more regular competitive fixtures with teams abroad. The men had their first World Cup in 1987, which cemented the idea in the heads of four women – Deborah Griffin, Sue Dorrington, Alice Cooper and Mary Forsyth – that a women's World Cup would be a truly excellent showcase of what the sport had achieved in recent years.

The four women gathered in the early mornings before work, at lunchtimes and after work to hatch a plan. They had little money or support, but they had an overwhelming desire to turn a brilliant idea into reality.

There were many logistical challenges in the beginning. The first being that before the age of social media or emails, it was hard to work out which unions had women's teams.

The organising committee knew that the USA, Canada, France, Netherlands, Spain and Sweden had teams, but were unsure of other countries. They wrote to them to ask if they had a women's team, and if that team would fancy playing at a World Cup. All correspondence was done via fax, Deborah recalls. She still has a file full of those messages. Even though the ink has long faded, Deborah wouldn't dare part with her folder of blank white pages that symbolise so much.

The committee used a sponsorship agency to help fulfil their promise to the visiting nations that they would cover all accommodation fees. Two months from the start date, the money had not been raised. Griffin and her co-organisers were left with no option but to sheepishly write to the unions to tell them that the inaugural Women's Rugby World Cup would have to be cancelled.

To their shock, each union wrote back to say they would still be coming. The four women realised that their mission to host the first Rugby World Cup had transformed into a mission held by players across the globe, all happy to dig into their own pockets to see the vision become a reality.

Cardiff was chosen to be the host city, due to its abundance of university accommodation, links to rugby and genuine desire to host the tournament. There was local support for the competition, as clubs across South Wales opened their doors to host matches and club members cheered along the touchline, but there wasn't any live broadcast interest, and only a little pick-up from national media. The Welsh Rugby Union provided referees for the tournament, clubs offered what they could, and players from different nations pulled together to make ends meet.

All that was left was to welcome the players and get the tournament started. The nine-day competition commenced with the opening ceremony. It was the first time that some of these international teams had met. The hard work was just about to begin, but for that night, there was celebration for the game and the shared passion that had brought them all together. A band played as teams marched in, some dressed smartly and some in tracksuits. People gave speeches and the event felt like a milestone in rugby union history.

The competition ran smoothly, despite atrocious weather at times and the most peculiar run-in with HMRC. The Soviet Union team arrived with no money or equipment to play rugby with. Unable to take money out of their country, the team arrived with arms full of vodka, dolls, caviar and cucumbers to haggle their way through the tournament. Their plan was to sell the goods on the streets of Cardiff, only for HMRC to knock on their door at the Cardiff Institute of Higher Education to tell them they could not do such a thing.

'The women were said to have travelled through Heathrow Airport's green channel with five 5ft cases of liquor, but at South Glamorgan Institute yesterday customs investigators found it almost impossible to break the language barrier and eventually left,' a *Guardian* report from 1991 reads. 'It is understood that no charges will be brought against the team, who had only enough money for their air fares and hoped to barter their goods for food during the week-long tournament in South Wales.'

The team managed to get by thanks to donations from the local community. A local store donated jerseys, another donated clothes and companies gave them money to help pay for their accommodation. Among other donations, a pie factory delivered produce to the players' accommodation to fuel them for the World Cup.

The team eventually finished the tournament with zero points to their name and left some debts for the hosts too. Even now, 30 years later, there is a raised eyebrow and pursed lips on the faces of the organisers when the Soviet team are mentioned. The story demonstrates just how hand to mouth the event was and how challenging it was for the organisers.

The tournament is best summarised by David Hands, rugby correspondent for *The Times* in 1991: 'The event, which reached its climax on Sunday in Cardiff when the United States beat England 19–6 in the final, has been run on a shoestring, with none of the trappings of the modern men's game – no big sponsors, no back-up, limited accommodation, but huge reserves of enthusiasm and considerable organisational skill.

'It was a tournament run for players by players who were prepared to risk their own money to bring their particular dream to fruition, and in that sense has taken rugby back to its original and purest roots.'

In fact 1991 is seen by many as the starting point for women's rugby history. Of course it was not, as this chapter has gone some way to describe and as previous written accounts have demonstrated. *Scrum Queens* by Ali Donnelly is the greatest source for a detailed delve into the history of the sport globally, and *World in Their Hands* by Martyn Thomas is a fantastic book about the 1991 World Cup.

This whistle-stop tour of women's rugby history in England does little justice to the rich stories of the most terrific women who made it their mission to shine a spotlight on the game, but should help acquaint readers with the women who fought tirelessly to get the game off the ground.

In 1994 it was decided that it was about time for another World Cup, this time hosted by the Netherlands, but the event organisers had not been granted official endorsement from the International Rugby Board (IRB) to title the event as the Women's Rugby World Cup. Minutes from the 1993 interim meeting of the IRB said they would 'defer consideration of participation by member unions in the tournament until such time as a formal request is received from the organisers'.

However, the next meeting for the IRB was not scheduled until days before the event was supposed to start, so the 'deferral' was essentially a refusal, as the event would not be sanctioned in time. As such, just 90 days before the event, the Netherlands pulled out. The World Cup had been cancelled.

The Scotland team received the fax just before a training session, which dampened spirits. After the session, they gathered in a pub in Leith and decided to host the tournament themselves. Sue Brodie, Scotland's full back and chairperson of the Scottish Women's Rugby Union, took the lead and gathered a team of volunteers to organise the tournament. Once again, the Women's Rugby World Cup was being organised by a small group of women. But this time it was named 'The Women's Rugby World Championship', because the IRB owned the trademark for the 'Rugby World Cup' title. As a technically unsanctioned event, the Netherlands and New Zealand did not attend and Spain pulled out at the last minute when their governing body refused to fund the trip.

The IRB even threatened sanctions against unions taking part in the unendorsed event but eventually 11 out of the original 16 teams turned out. Regardless of the thrown-together nature, some rugby heavyweights were in action, including England, the USA (who were of course the reigning champions at the time), Canada and France.

The first great high for the Red Roses came on 24 April 1994. England had enjoyed a smooth and successful journey into the World Cup final and would face the USA once again.

Giselle Mather, Red Rose number 35, woke up on that morning in The George Hotel in Edinburgh and whipped open the curtains. She could see the top of the rugby posts at the Edinburgh Academicals. In a few hours, she would be playing a World Cup final on that pitch. And she woke up with pure clarity: today is the day she becomes a world champion. Giselle got changed into her travelling clothes and plugged in her Sony Walkman. It had become somewhat of a match-day tradition to listen to Bon Jovi as she prepared for the match. It was one part of her personal warm-up routine – as integral as the tube of Smarties (the orange ones saved until last, always) or the juggling. Three juggling balls were in every bag she packed for a rugby match. Never dropping a rugby ball was the cornerstone of Giselle's game, a crucial skill to have as an international back heading into a World Cup final. So in her hotel room stood Giselle, with her short spiky hair, juggling three balls and thinking about the day ahead. Soon it was time to leave, and Giselle got on the bus with her team, some of her best friends scattered across the seats. Everyone was thinking about the game, but Giselle was confident they would win. They had beaten the USA the year before. While their backs were skilful, the forwards were technically shabby and she knew England would power past them.

Giselle was proved right, and the Red Roses became world champions for the first time, beating the United States 38–23. The celebrations – which included commandeering a fire engine – began. There was no suggestion of this being an unofficial title. Unsanctioned, maybe, but this was the World Cup and it was treated with the respect it deserved.

Giselle left the hotel on the Monday morning, having settled the £1,800 bill for her stay. Each player had paid their own way to the World Cup and the team had decided to stay at The George Hotel despite it being expensive, because it was known for hosting rugby teams and felt special. Fit for World Cup winners, even.

A key part of that World Cup-winning England squad was Gill Burns, a force to be reckoned with on the pitch who was a main member of the England squad in those early days. Gill was a good dancer, thanks to her mum Ann being a dance teacher, a promising runner (100 metres in 12 seconds) and enjoyed all sports. After only playing five rugby matches, Gill was called up to the England squad and became a driving force in the organisation of England vs Sweden at her home club of Firwood Waterloo, near Liverpool, in 1988. One 'alickadoo', as Gill so brilliantly describes him, said to her, 'Gill, I came here in the hope of seeing some tits and bums, but after five minutes I was watching a bloody good game of rugger.' He went on to enjoy a drink in the club bar, but Gill couldn't join him there. Despite organising an England international at the club, Gill had to abide by the sign on the door of the bar: 'No women and no dogs allowed'.

It's a glimpse back in time when Gill confronted sexism often. In her house is a treasure trove of women's rugby history, with bookshelves full of scrapbooks detailing her rugby career. In one, she is photographed playing rugby in a tutu. It was a condition imposed by the newspaper of running the interview: she had to be in a tutu, or the interview wouldn't run. So Gill did it, recognising that the need to get the message of women's rugby out there was more important than her personal pride. 'I genuinely don't remember, in the early days, complaining about things,' Gill says. 'We were grateful because we had the opportunity to play this wonderful sport. And yes, we weren't getting the same as the fellas and we weren't getting watched by enough people. But if we thought about that too much, if we'd focused on things we weren't getting, it wouldn't have been fun.'

Nearly all the coverage from that era is patronising at best, sexist at worst. There are a few exceptions: male allies in journalism who took women's rugby seriously and covered it with respect. Then there were the tabloids, who liked to present the players as drinkers, or made it all sound like it was all just a bit of fun.

Gill played every minute of every game from that match against Sweden in 1988, up until the 1998–99 season. Every minute, except when she left the pitch during one match for a few minutes to have her eyebrow stitched back together. For that, she can be excused. Gill eventually retired in 2002.

The England women's rugby team has changed significantly since Gill and Giselle's days. There are professional contracts, and players do not need to work full-time jobs and lose money to play for England. Yet Gill would not change any of it for the world.

'Through my 14 years of playing for England, when we started off, there were probably four or five world-class players in the England team,' Gill says. 'When I finished there were probably eight or ten world-class players in the England team. Now there are 30 world-class players, 40, 50 world-class players in the England set-up; that's the difference. It's the strength index that's made them so much better. It's the fact that people are looked after, the fact that people are professional. That is the key. I would never ever change my days and I thoroughly enjoyed every minute of the hardships. It was really enjoyable, and the whole thing was fantastic, but I am intrigued. I would love to know what sort of athlete I could have become if I'd had the support that the girls have now.'

Those early years are crucial in the history of the Red Roses. For so many years, women's rugby was completely amateur and a far cry from the professional set-up England enjoy today. The history teaches a wonderful lesson in women working together to get things done and not letting anybody stop them. In 2009, the IRB recognised the 1991 and 1994 World Cups as official tournaments at the bottom of a press release about the 2010 World Cup. Though it was in spite of the governing body and not thanks to them, the official endorsement of the tournaments was gratefully received by all players, and ended any debate over whether they really counted as World Cups.

The former (or 'vintage' as they like to be known) Red Roses wrote their history long before the Rugby Football Union did and kept track of each cap so every player knew what number Red Rose they were. It's not always been easy and there have been debates over the order of the list and memories so faded that games overlap and details are confused. But thanks to that hard work, the Red Roses now have a definitive list of the women who have represented England. In 2023, ahead of the fixture against France in their first ever stand-alone fixture at Twickenham Stadium, a wall was unveiled with the full list of every Red Rose, to match the men's list in the stadium.

Today's players are reminded of the team's history regularly, and often name former Red Roses in conversation. It might be that they were taught by one, as current Roses Holly Aitchison and Sarah Beckett were taught at school by Gill, or it might be a passing conversation at a rugby event. Or, it might be the likes of Claudia MacDonald, Maud Muir and Abby Dow, who were coached by Giselle at Wasps and credit a lot of their talent to the lessons taught by the legend.

Women's rugby players have had to fight for all their history. For the chance to play the sport they love and for the game to love them back. Rugby union builds its values on respect, but for many years it did not respect the women's game and that must be acknowledged before we move on to the time rugby caught up with what the women were up to. It's no coincidence that as we track the progression of women's rugby, the peaks match with the waves of feminism.

Today's players are still pushing for more, as they should. They want better pay and better conditions and they want girls to have better access to rugby in schools. Sue Day, former Red Rose and current chief financial officer and chief operations officer at the RFU, believes they are entitled to ask for more, even though it is not always possible. But on they push, because if the history of women's rugby teaches players anything, it's that there is no credit in being grateful for scraps.

Chapter 2

GROWING ROSES

Women's rugby developed into the 21st century, with small hubs of women's rugby players growing around the country. One was at Oldfield Academy in Bath, where 16-year-old boys and girls could go and study for their A levels alongside training in a high-performance environment. The women were coached by Gary Street, who would go on to become England's head coach, and his young students included future Red Roses Rachael Burford, Danielle 'Nolli' Waterman, Heather Fisher, Claire Allan and Kat Merchant. When they didn't have lessons, they would be training on the rugby pitches. It was a very early form of a high-performance environment, with the players living away from home and fully embedded in a rugby academy.

Gary remembers how Rachael would spend hours every single day perfecting her pass, dragging him out of his office to do passing training, even if the pair had already spent two hours practising the same techniques that morning. In 2001, Gary took the team to the European 7s competition and upon arrival the players were shocked to see the pitch had been made shorter and narrower for the women. They had to play with inflatable rugby posts which crossed over in the wind, challenging any attempt at a successful conversion.

By the time of the 2006 World Cup, there was a bank of talent not only in the England team but also on the fringes, with the England academy now set up and working well to produce talented Red Roses. The international game by this point had more support from the IRB (now World Rugby), but England were still being run by the Rugby Football Union for Women (RFUW), which was not fully absorbed by the RFU until 2010.

The support was small in 2006 and England received the vast majority of their funding from Sport England. There was one tackle that effectively saved women's rugby in England, according to Gary. In 2006, as he recalls, the team would have lost their Sport England funding had they not reached the Rugby World Cup final. Gary decided not to tell the players or his coaching staff what was riding on their performances, so as not to add to the pressure on them.

In the semi-final, against Canada, England maintained a comfortable lead late into the second half and Gary felt calmer in the stands. For now, his England women's rugby programme was safe. But all of a sudden, two quick tries from Canada put England's safety into question. With the score 20–14, Canada were within one try of beating England and battling their way into the final. Canada got a scrum deep in their own half but, with England's defence tiring after an end-to-end match, the Canadian backs decided to run with the ball, beating the foot chase of the Red Roses and nearing the touchline when winger Kim Shaylor took down her Canadian opponent just in front of the try line. That one tackle meant England won the game, sent them through to the final and, unbeknown to Kim, saved England's women's rugby programme.

England lost the final to New Zealand in 2006, adding one more chapter into what has become the biggest rivalry in women's rugby. Four years later, in 2010, Gary was the England head coach and the team had won all four Six Nations tournaments since the previous World Cup, including three Grand Slams. England were hosting the tournament and were on good form to win, when New Zealand, once more, beat them in a hard-fought final.

Ahead of 2014, Gary knew he had to expose the players to New Zealand more. The tournaments were often decided against New Zealand and the Red Roses sat them on a pedestal in their heads. The Black Ferns were their biggest rivals and the Six Nations was not providing England with the competition needed to prepare them for those all-or-nothing matches against the Black Ferns. So in 2011 and 2012, England helped fund the Black Ferns to play in two three-Test series, and England travelled to New Zealand in 2013 to play a return series there. In 2011, England won two and drew one, in 2012 England won all three and in 2013 they lost all three. For Gary, that 2013 series was when he knew England would win the 2014 World Cup, because England had got close to the Black Ferns without their strongest side (some of the leading England players could not get the time off work to travel to New Zealand), and he could see how his players reacted under pressure.

In the years between 2010 and 2014, Gary had also started to train his England team against men's academy teams who were much quicker and, crucially, were very fast off the defensive line – a key part of New Zealand's game that England had struggled to replicate in training scenarios. The training camps had become truly brutal as well. The hardest day of the week was 'Toughen-up Tuesday'. The players took a 'beasting', Gary describes, in a horrendous physical and mental challenge. The players did a gruelling amount of strength and conditioning work before being split into two teams and playing a match. The team knew that selection decisions could be based on their performances in that match and they gave everything in those sessions, despite being physically exhausted. Everyone would be knackered, replicating how bodies often feel in a World Cup final, and Gary was testing who could make good decisions under that pressure.

In matches, Gary had rotated his squad so that every player was gaining valuable experience. When the 2014 World Cup squad of 26 was announced, his strongest XV had an average of 50 caps and the rest had an average of 33. The team had also taken some professional contracts before the tournament which had helped them prepare as best they could. 'It just felt different,' Emily Scarratt reflects. 'In terms of the preparation, the training we had done, I think we just felt like we were the best prepared we could possibly be, so if it wasn't to be it wasn't because we hadn't done everything right.' By the time the World Cup, hosted in France, came around, Gary felt confident that his team would lift the trophy, but it wasn't without one final spanner in the works that threatened everything.

England arrived at their training base in France on good form. Gary had transported the entire women's gym from Twickenham to France, including the floor, wall fittings and every piece of equipment. Everything had been carefully placed in the exact same spots so that the players felt familiar with their surroundings. There had been considerable effort put in by Gary and his staff to make the environment feel homely, but one thing they could not predict was a group of armed travellers surrounding their camp. On the eve of the World Cup, England were on the cusp of having to leave and go home, afraid for their safety. The government's sports minister at the time had to step in and England were given an armed escort to take them in and out of the camp.

As the tournament began on 1 August 2014, Gary stuck to his game plan and made mass changes between matches to replicate how England had prepared for the tournament. In the pool stages, England comprehensively beat Samoa and Spain, 65–3 and 45–5 respectively, and drew 13–13 with Canada. New Zealand had an awful pool stage, losing to Ireland and not qualifying for the semi-finals. At the time, the BBC described it as 'the biggest shock in the history of the competition'. England's greatest rival had been overcome, but they would now have to face a triumphant Ireland in the semi-final. It proved to be a storming success for the Red Roses, who won 40–7 and set up a final against Canada, whom they had reached a stalemate with in the pool stages.

If you had opened the wrong door and accidentally stumbled into the training camp in the week that followed, you would have no idea this was a team preparing for a World Cup final. The staff tried to keep the pressure off the team by remaining calm and sticking to their routine.

In the 74th minute, the Red Roses were pushing hard in a maul and eventually the ball came to Natasha 'Mo' Hunt, the scrum half, at the back, who shipped it to fly half and team captain Katy McLean (now Katy Daley-McLean). Katy has no trouble admitting there was no game plan here, but it's never a bad idea to pass the ball to Emily Scarratt. Emily handed off a defender and created the space in front of her to cross the line, all but confirming the World Cup. Emily completed her scoring for the day by landing the conversion, taking her personal points tally for the day to 16.

The final whistle blew and after 20 years, England had won the World Cup. The celebrations that evening, that night, and long into the following morning, were legendary. Captain Katy was known to have stopped players who were trying to sneak off to bed, and at one point 'put her life on the line' (reports may be exaggerated) to save the World Cup from the swimming pool. As the team bus left the stadium, they spotted a pub on a roundabout which had been commandeered by England's supporters. In that pub were the players' families, their fans and former Red Roses. The staff decided to stop the bus and the players were told they had five minutes to greet their fans. As the team got off the bus, the pub's occupants spilled on to the street and greeted them with a chorus of 'Swing Low, Sweet Chariot'. Two and a half hours later they were still drinking. There was no telling these players to go home, especially when they didn't have to buy themselves a single drink.

The team had been on professional contracts for the tournament, but this was a success built in the amateur years of rugby. 'Amateur' is a loaded word. Of course, for many years that's exactly what the Red Roses were. They were a team of women juggling careers and family life with playing international rugby. They were amateur because they were unpaid, but the dedication of the team was nothing short of professional.

While I was studying for my politics degree at Swansea University, the head of rugby was Siwan Lillicrap, who was a Wales player at the time and would go on to be the Wales captain. Siwan had a full-time job and played for Swansea RFC, the Ospreys and Wales. I will always remember a chat with her in her office one day, when she told me about her week. It involved working full-time, coaching on some evenings, training on others and playing rugby at the weekend. She might be playing for any one of her three teams, but if she was playing for Wales it involved travelling to the training base in Cardiff and flying out to whichever country Wales were playing in that weekend. World Cups involved taking annual leave from work and Siwan would often be back at her desk on a Monday morning after playing rugby for Wales at the weekend. If that conversation with Siwan hadn't happened, there's a good chance this book would not have been written, by me anyway. It inspired me to write about the sacrifices women make to play in the Six Nations, and that year I wrote my first piece for *The Times*, while on work experience on the sports desk. The title was: 'I basically live in my car' – the sacrifices women make to play in the Six Nations.

Earlier that week, another journalist had suggested that the Women's Six Nations fixtures should be moved to a Wednesday night to avoid clashing with the men's championship. It felt so short-sighted to me. Players would have to take at least three days of annual leave for away matches and would have perhaps no time to rest.

For many players, and for many years, the reality of

playing rugby for their country was to juggle the impossible task of working or studying alongside rugby. Elinor Snowsill, the Wales fly half, remembers wearing compression socks in work on a Monday after playing for Wales at the weekend to help her body recover from Test-level rugby. 'I'm on my feet all day at work and then I have training, but the biggest challenge is the mental one,' she told me back in 2019. 'I might have a challenging day in work, say a safeguarding issue, and then I have to be mentally switched on in the evenings for training, too. It's a lot of balls to keep juggling. It can get quite stressful.

'As amateurs we can still train as much, we just do it in the mornings and nights [before and after work]. It's the recovery time that is the biggest difference,' she says. 'I wear compression socks and I try to get to a swimming pool, but obviously it's not the same.'

When Katy turned full-time professional with England in 2019, she reflected that the additional time given to recover was the best part. 'I have a better work-life balance now,' she told me. 'Before, when I was a primary school teacher, I'd have to go into work the day after playing for England, but now I have time to recover and spend time with my family. We're getting out of camp and spending time at home and we can use that time wisely to put our feet up without the worry of having to squeeze work in. Now, I can get up and have breakfast, go to the gym, come back, have some lunch, go do a skills session, and then go to club training. It makes my day a lot more pleasant.'

In January 2019, England announced that 28 Red Roses would turn full-time professional. It was a turning point not only for the team but for women's rugby globally. It shifted the dial and the performances that followed demonstrated the benefits of such an investment.

But it's easy to forget how tough it was for England players for such a long time. The contract situation with England had been messy since the first ones were introduced ahead of the 2014 Rugby World Cup. The breaking point for many Red Roses came in the summer of 2018. After a few years of full-time contracts being spoken of, and managing to get by with full-time jobs, juggling part-time deals or sevens contracts, the players felt left in the dark over the contract situation. In August, just a month away from the start of the 2018–19 season, the players did not know crucial details about the contracts for the forthcoming season, including how much they would be worth, or if they would be part-time or full-time deals. The lack of information led a number of players to consider not signing new contracts at all.

One player who was there at the time remembers the bleakness of the situation. 'There was a lack of trust in the RFU at that point,' she says. 'We just didn't know what was going on and players would send articles from the media in group chats which had different information about our contracts than what we had been told. We were told we might have to train on more days, which was tough for those of us who had jobs, and the money wouldn't have been enough for people to quit [their] jobs to focus on rugby. It was already a huge commitment and we were scared that if we didn't sign the contracts, we wouldn't play for England ever again. When you're playing rugby, all you want to do is play for England and when that might be taken from you it's scary. So scary. I wouldn't say I was scared of the management but I was certainly apprehensive about my commitments and my family were telling me to focus on my career and retire from rugby.'

It reached the point where players were considering strike action, putting an autumn series in doubt, but the players decided against striking when it was agreed behind closed doors that professional, full-time contracts in the XVs game would be introduced. Nevertheless, by the time the resolution had been found, some players had given up their careers or turned down promotions to play for England.

The year before, in 2017, the team reached another crisis point while training at Bisham Abbey ahead of a three-Test autumn series. The team had just lost the 2017 Rugby World Cup final and the RFU chose not to renew contracts, leaving many having to go part-time with rugby. England Rugby had instead chosen to focus on the sevens game, and those who did not take a sevens contract were presented with part-time deals worth £900 a match, plus £1,400 for being in the squad.

Players who were in the XVs squad at the time report that they were shut in a room and handed contracts that they had to sign in order to be allowed to train. 'There was a lot of emotion in the room,' a source told *The Times* back in 2018. 'There were players in tears, players who were angry. These were big decisions.' The players agreed to refuse to sign the contracts and to seek advice from the Rugby Players' Association and independent lawyers. The day's training session, the only contact training session before the first Test against Canada, was cancelled. 'No one was allowed to do any kind of a walk-through; you weren't allowed a rugby ball in your hand; you couldn't do anything rugby-related until the contracts had been signed,' the source said.

The same year, players were discussing crowdfunding to cover their expenses and to help them manage work alongside playing for England. Players say that they were told to drop the idea because of the negative publicity that could follow such a move. 'Mentally and physically it broke quite a lot of players, last year [in 2017],' a source told *The Times*. 'It pushed people to the edge. Everyone is desperate to play for their country and will give up everything.

'That's what hurts the most: this continual expectation from the RFU that the players will just agree to it because they always have. It shouldn't be like that. Everybody has been stressed by this. It affects your life. There isn't a single person in the squad who doesn't feel that at the moment.'

Marlie Packer remembers her experiences well: 'I was one of the first players to ever get a contract in 2013,' she recalls. 'Which was a part-time contract. Then when we were on the bus on the way to the 2014 World Cup, I signed one of the first ever sevens full-time contracts, which is the most bizarre thing because we're on the way to a 15-a-side World Cup but we were signing our contracts on the bus. Well, you had to sign it before you got on the bus. There were only so many players who had the contract, but yeah we needed to do that. And then from 2014 to 2017 I was fully employed by the RFU.

'I didn't get selected for Rio [Olympics, 2016], so they changed my contract from sevens to XVs, and then my contract ended the same as everyone else's in 2017, but I was working for HomeServe at the time, so I stayed employed by them until 2019.' Marlie, who formerly worked as a plumber and level three gas engineer, was one of the 28 players who took a full-time deal in 2019.

In response to the allegations from players published in *The Times*, an RFU spokeswoman said: 'We have a good relationship and regular dialogue with the group who represent the women's XVs players. Our position has been consistent and clear – our *ambition* is to introduce women's XVs contracts and we will do it as soon as it is possible and financially sustainable, which is what we outlined earlier this week. If we can introduce contracts this season, we will – but we are still reviewing what is possible.

'We are disappointed to hear allegations about the culture within the women's team camp. If any of the players have any issues or complaints, we encourage them to tell us and we will deal with it. We have a new 'speak up' policy which encourages players if they want to speak out about anything, and we take our duty of care very seriously.'

In September 2018, one month after players were considering strike action, the RFU announced the 28 full-time central contracts for the squad plus seven part-time contracts known as Elite Player Squad agreements. The contracts would start on 1 January 2019, and the RFU committed to making the deals permanent. This gave players the assurance that they would not need to move between the sevens and the XVs sides, as both squads would now be fully professional. The full-time deals were originally worth £20,000–30,000, enough for players to make the decision about leaving other employment to focus on rugby, and in 2023 the salaries were reported as being worth upwards of £26,000–£34,000, plus match fees of £800 per match, giving in-form players the chance to boost their earnings with match appearances. The contracts ended the uncertainty that had been in place since the 2017 Rugby World Cup.

It was a sour start to life as professionals but players say that the unrest felt in the year from the 2017 World Cup to the professional contracts being announced in September 2018 was soon dissolved as they focused on the new start. It felt like a clean slate, and a chance to lead the way globally as the only women in the world in a full-time professional XVs programme.

It started a trend in rugby of women's teams moving to professional models. The goalposts had been moved and for other countries to keep up with England, and the part-time programmes in New Zealand and France, they now had to invest. Scotland awarded contracts to eight players who had the specific focus of helping the team qualify for the 2021 World Cup.

Pressure mounted on other countries to invest in their own programmes, with money slowly dripping into the system in the run-up to the 2021 World Cup. Perhaps most notably was the investment by the Welsh Rugby Union (WRU). A year out from the World Cup, they announced that ten players would become full-time professionals and a further 15 would be on retainer contracts in the squad. The deals were believed to be worth around £19,000 and described as 'not life-changing' by Nigel Walker, the WRU's director of performance. The move came after Jasmine 'Jaz' Joyce, the Team GB sevens star and Wales XVs player, tweeted about having to return to work as a personal trainer and teacher trainee after her sevens contract was due to run out in December 2021. 'I love being part of Great Britain and playing on the world series, but unfortunately after the Dubai [World Rugby Sevens] Series in December, it [the funding and contracts] will go back to England,' Joyce wrote on social media. 'Meaning I will no longer be living the dream as a full-time rugby player, but balancing both a full-time job and rugby.'

Again, players were advocating for themselves in order to get their unions to invest. Jaz's words were echoed across the world as senior women's players publicly called on their unions to invest in the women's teams. England had led the way, and with a World Cup looming on the horizon, talks of contracts bloomed and more nations turned semi-professional or full-time professional ahead of the World Cup.

Since England's professional contracts were introduced, the level of professionalism in England has developed to an unrecognisable set-up which has revolutionised women's rugby. Players now have access to nutritionists, strength and conditioning coaches, a psychologist, an analyst and more. Chapters four and five will delve deeper into the logistics of life as a professional women's rugby player, but above all the support and financial backing behind England's success, it is the women in the team that make it the force they are.

Chapter 3

IT TAKES A CERTAIN KIND
OF WOMAN

The Red Roses are women who would succeed in any area of life. Thank God, for us anyway, they chose rugby. But what does it take to play women's rugby for England? As the game develops, especially at the grassroots level, becoming a Red Rose has become harder and the competition greater than ever.

The journey for all players begins in childhood, even if they didn't pick up a rugby ball until much later. The Red Roses tend to say that playing a variety of sports while young made them better players. Netball can give you good hand-eye coordination, cricket can help players catch, football helps kicking, and all sports help you to develop the skills of tactical awareness and reading a game.

There are, of course, socioeconomic factors that come into play. Parents have to pay for sports clubs and have to be able to take the players to training sessions and games, and children who go to private schools tend to have greater access to rugby from a younger age, better facilities, and more advanced PE lessons thanks to the higher staff-to-student ratio. Rugby is traditionally a middle-class and upper-class sport, and despite efforts to change its public image, it might not appeal to those from lower socioeconomic classes who feel they would not fit in.

Once the players are playing rugby, they must develop their skills to become technically excellent in their position. They must have full ownership of fundamental rugby skills like passing and tackling. Mentally, players aspiring to represent England must demonstrate they have the ability to deal with the pressure of playing rugby in a Test-level environment. They should show dedication and commitment to their development, be competitive in a challenging sport, and be able to play well as part of a team. Players can progress through grassroots teams, local leagues, counties and academies before breaking into the Allianz Premiership Women's Rugby, the top league in England and the most competitive league in the world.

The coaches spread themselves across Premiership Women's Rugby matches to scout out talent. 'We look for if they can cope in the Premiership Women's Rugby in their primary position,' Louis Deacon, the England forwards coach, explains. 'Can they do their primary role really well? Is she standing out? Is she finding any parts of her game difficult? And is there an opportunity for them to improve?'

Whereas current generations of young girls have an abundance of wonderful women's rugby players from diverse backgrounds to look to as role models, many of the current Red Roses were not aware of the women's rugby players who came before them in the early days of their careers. Girls today are also far more likely to have access to good quality coaching and women's rugby content to consume on their phones. Nearly every Red Rose has a story of being told that rugby isn't for girls, of being told to stop playing by coaches, and of boys refusing to pass to them. So for the current crop of Roses, their journey to reach the top of women's rugby required the strong will to keep going despite the roadblocks in their way.

Of course it requires dedication to reach the top of any sport. Many sportspeople go on to have incredibly successful careers in other spheres of life, thanks in part to the skills they learned in sport. It takes a certain kind of person to excel in sport and part of that is being ruthless, difficult and often selfish. Former Olympic champion Sir Bradley Wiggins explains it best: 'The thing with sport is, at a high level like that, you are encouraged to be narcissistic,' he said in a *Times* interview. 'You're praised for it. Sport is the only industry in the world where you are praised to be narcissistic.'

The focus on improving tiny aspects of your game and honing your craft requires dedication. Elite sport chisels players into sharp people able to perform at the highest level. It enables people to manage their lives with the focus of personal development. It can make people selfish, but it also makes them incredibly driven.

Playing rugby takes courage and requires being able to face your fears and do it anyway. But playing rugby as a woman requires being happy to place yourself in male-dominated spaces and thrive. That might be playing in boys-only teams as a child or turning up to rugby clubs full of men in blazers and demanding the women get to play on the first-team pitch. To rise to the top of the game, you must prove yourself relentlessly and advocate for yourself constantly without giving in.

Nearly every Red Rose has a story of boys not passing the ball to them, of facing abuse from other players' parents or dealing with toffee-nosed people who do not want to support women and girls playing rugby. A particular favourite memory is from Sarah Bern. As a youngster, she turned up to a rugby tournament and overheard a coach suggesting she wouldn't be good enough to be in the team with the boys. So she waited until he was on the tackle pad and sent him flying six foot backwards.

Rugby also teaches those values the sport sits so perilously on. There is camaraderie, teamwork and, of course, respect. The team culture in the current England squad means there are no narcissists, nobody close to what Sir Bradley described. It's not quite as explicit as the All Blacks' famous 'no dickheads' policy, but it's a team of women who support one another and are not afraid to be vulnerable in front of each other. The result is a team of highly-skilled women with skills transferable to the outside world.

There are women like Claudia MacDonald, who got ten A*s and one A at GCSE, three A*s at A level and an economics degree from Durham University. Ellie Kildunne and Helena Rowland were completing university assignments during the 2023 Six Nations. In fact, at England training camps there is often a table of players with their laptops open and their headphones in, completing work from their other jobs or typing up university assignments. The players know that rugby will not last forever, and it doesn't earn them enough to enjoy a comfortable retirement either.

Here are the stories of four women who had different paths to becoming Red Roses.

Marlie Packer

Marlie Packer turned up to her first rugby training session aged six in jeans and a red top with frills around the neck and the arms. 'It weren't a bit of me, Jess,' she says in her thick West Country accent as she describes the outfit she hated so much. Her friend's parents had taken Marlie to the training session after school, and Marlie's mum had assumed that her daughter was just going to watch, not play. She had quite the shock when young Marlie came home covered in mud. The red top was now completely brown and had to be chucked away, much to Marlie's delight.

The training session had been so much fun. At school, Marlie had played hockey and rounders but had to give netball a miss because she was too aggressive. As she grew up and became a teenager, football became another great love of Marlie's and she played at Yeovil Town Ladies football club until the under-16s. For years, on a Saturday was football and a Sunday was rugby. Then when Marlie turned 16 and joined the senior women's football team at Yeovil, she faced a tough choice. Her football fixtures would now be on a Sunday, clashing with her rugby. The choice between the two sports felt like the biggest decision in her life at the time. The coaches at the football club were all women whom Marlie idolised, but rugby was where she expressed herself. She loved the safe place to use her aggression – a characteristic that was frowned upon in other sports – and whether she will admit it or not, she also so clearly had the gift. Her football coaches still tell her that she could have risen to the top of football, too, but she doesn't believe them. Rugby was the sport for Marlie.

Before long, Marlie left school and was being encouraged to study sports courses at college, so she learned to coach kids. She hated it. Mainly because at the time she really wasn't too fond of children, but also because she had to coach on Tuesdays, Thursdays and Saturdays, which were the days she trained for rugby. Her interest was piqued by more physical jobs and in the summers and half-term breaks at college, Marlie had been doing some labouring for bricklayers. Around the same time, she had been called up to the England under-20s, where a rugby advisor called Zoe Eaton stepped in to help work out the next steps. Plumbing was a particular interest of Marlie's, so Zoe helped Marlie apply for a plumbing apprenticeship.

While starting that apprenticeship in 2008, the first senior call-up to England arrived. It was two and a half weeks away in a camp and she felt so lonely that she called her mum every day. Marlie remembers the England camps being an uninviting place and now when someone new enters the camp she goes to considerable effort to make sure they don't feel the same way. She knew nobody in the camp and felt daunted enough to decide to stick with the under-20s for as long as possible rather than take the step up to the senior team.

When you think of Marlie Packer the rugby player, it's hard to imagine her feeling in such a way.

On the pitch, she is a commanding presence who wallops through defence and screams instructions at the top of her lungs. She's not been shy of an on-pitch confrontation with her opponents, and tackles with no fear for herself. When watching England, it's not unusual to see her pop up from under a ruck, brush her unruly hair out of her eyes, and race to the next ruck while tightening whichever few strands of her hair are left in her bun.

There's a tightrope between aggression and anger which Marlie storms across. Jess Breach, a team-mate at Saracens who played against her for some time while the winger was at Harlequins, remembers being nervous to play against Marlie and a bit intimidated by her, before they got to know each other.

I wonder if having her son, Oliver, was the catalyst for Marlie's kindness, but her team-mates say that while Oliver has brought out her best qualities, she has always been a friendly face in the camp. The Marlie off the pitch is very different to the player. She is calm and kind. She offers me a lift when I visit her at her Saracens training centre to save me the long walk from the gym to my car, moving aside Oliver's toys to make room for me. When I go into the England camps to observe, Marlie makes sure I know where the coffee machine is and checks that I'm happy. In short, she thinks about the small things that could make me feel more comfortable – introductions to people I hadn't met, for example – and goes to some effort for me without being asked. Two days before England played France at Twickenham Stadium at the 2023 Women's Six Nations, Marlie offered to take an England shirt of mine and get it signed by the whole squad then return it to me when she saw me next. I refused to add any extra burden in a week she was captaining England in a Grand Slam decider, but the gesture was gratefully received. There's a kindness that goes above what I expected from her and I get a good sense of what it would be like if I was a player going into camp. It would be reductionist to say she is the mum of the camp, but it's clear that Marlie wants to make sure no England player ever feels how she did when she first entered the England set-up.

Marlie is also one of the most emotional players in the squad. There are a few topics that bring tears to her eyes. She openly talks about her struggles growing up and believes that she had two roads she could have gone down in life, and rugby kept her on the right path. She's unsure where the other road would have led her – she doesn't want to know – but she believes rugby gave her the right support to work hard and achieve all she has.

Marlie's father was largely absent in her life. He was in and out of prison for much of his life, and only really connected with Marlie once she was in her late teens. Her mum, Julie, filled the gap her father had left, along with Marlie's grandad. Julie shipped Marlie to all her after-school activities and spent her weekends taking her to football and rugby. Julie never said no and would do all she could for Marlie and her brother. 'I miss my dad and I do think about him, of course I do, but I'm angry as well,' Marlie said in a *World Rugby* interview with Ugo Monye. 'For me, I would never choose anything but to be there for Oliver. Spend time with him, take him swimming. To see him grow. Sometimes I watch him sleep and I just want to pick him up. I just don't understand how someone couldn't be like that with me. So now I feel like, with my dad, I'm a little bit angry at the situation because I'm now a parent, and he didn't see me win a World Cup and he hasn't seen me become a parent. That, mixed in with stuff, makes me angry. But at the same time, they were his life choices not mine.'

Her father passed away twelve weeks before the 2014

Rugby World Cup, which was a tough time for Marlie. But since having Oliver, the pain of how her father treated her has hit her more than ever before. She thinks about all she does for Oliver, and it makes her even more grateful for all that her own mum did for her as a child. There's anger towards her father, but there's also grief.

What Oliver has brought into Marlie's life is a renewed sense of purpose. When she talks of Oliver's *Peppa Pig* obsession and love of dinosaurs, there's no sense of the rugby player any more. This is a working mum who is doing all she can to give her son the best life and make him proud of her. She is relatable and relaxed.

At the time of Marlie's first cap, playing for England was unpaid, other than a £50 payment for loss of earnings and travel expenses, so she decided to focus on finishing her apprenticeship and continue playing in the under-20s. In the young squad she was a big fish in a small pond, compared to a small fish in a very big pond when she was with the senior team. It wasn't until 2012, when Marlie had finished her apprenticeship, that she got her second senior England cap, three years and three months after her first call-up.

Life had changed quite a lot in those three years. Marlie had come out as gay and was in her first relationship with a woman, called Kate. She was happier and more confident in herself. To Marlie, Kate appeared to have the perfect family. She used to call their home a doll's house because it seemed perfect: two windows upstairs, two downstairs, and a door in the middle. Kate's parents, who were childhood sweethearts, had worked really hard for everything they had which gave Marlie new role models. Spending time with

Kate's family made two things clear: she wanted to work hard so she could own her own house, and she wanted to have a family. Marlie achieved both of those things, and despite her accolades in rugby, owning her own home and raising Oliver are the two achievements closest to her heart because she knows how hard she has had to work for it. Although Marlie and Kate are separated they have remained friends, and Kate's nana and grandad still come to watch Marlie play rugby.

In terms of rugby, the 2014 Rugby World Cup win is the most precious of her achievements, but it took losing the 2021 World Cup for Marlie to realise just how special 2014 really was. Back then, she was 24 and felt like her and Alex Matthews were the kids on tour, there for a good time, having fun, and then all of a sudden they won the World Cup. She reflects that perhaps she was too young to realise what the win meant to her at the time. The 2017 World Cup final was won by New Zealand, who Marlie concedes were the better team on the day. It's the 2021 final that hurts the most. 'New Zealand didn't win it, we lost it,' she says. England let the match slip, and it's something that Marlie finds difficult to talk about. She was 33 then and at the top of her game, but the medal wasn't to be hers.

Older, calmer and happier, Marlie Packer the England captain is an entirely different woman to the young player who first joined the England senior camp. She cannot resist dancing every time she hears 'Flowers' by Miley Cyrus, even if that interrupts a gym session, and isn't afraid to look silly if it entertains her team-mates.

She has built her own happiness. Nothing in life has ever been handed to Marlie. Her driving force is to defy expectations of herself and to make her family proud. There's always a plan for what the next goal is, and right now, the goal is to run out at the Rugby World Cup final in 2025 with Oliver, who will be four and a half by then, at her side. She knows there are younger players ready to take her shirt, so she keeps on top of her game, raising the bar and remembering what keeps her motivated.

Maud Muir

'We aren't the best team in the world until we have won the World Cup,' barked England head coach Simon Middleton, to a room with mixed expressions. There were only three months to go until the 2021 Rugby World Cup and the team were in the midst of a training camp at Bath University, all desperate to prove their worth to the coaches, who were using these training camps as a chance to narrow down their squad selection for the flight to New Zealand.

The 'Thorns', the name given to the Red Roses' leadership group, were spread across the front rows. Among them sat Marlie Packer, Sarah Hunter and Abbie Ward. Marlie's face is cold, her eyebrows pushed together, as she listens to Simon. Sarah looks relaxed, because she knows what Simon will say. She has been here many times before. Abbie looks focused and confident. All three understood that a 23-match winning streak would not appease a coach so focused on lifting the trophy.

Nearer the back of the room was Maud Muir, the 20-year-old prop at the beginning of her Red Roses journey. Her eyes didn't move from Simon, tracing his every step around the room and absorbing his speech.

The day before, the squad had completed their toughest training day of the World Cup preparation so far. The team had been split into mixed groups of forwards and backs and had to work as a team to sprint from cone to cone, completing a set number of exercises at each station. The group could only move on when everyone in the team had finished their exercises. Maud had found this a challenge but her team did not finish last, which was a huge reassurance for her. As she has grown in the team, Maud has become used to not settling. The standards in the squad had been set by the players around her, and the drive to come first in every race or training activity had developed the competitive edge needed to play in the number one rugby team in the world. Winning is the number one priority of the Red Roses, always. Nothing else will do.

The intensity of the week's training sessions had given Maud a sense of just how tough it would be to play at a World Cup, but even at the tender age of 20, the young prop had already proved herself as a hard worker, someone willing to put in the extra work, and it translated into her becoming a valuable member of the squad.

Maud grew up in Oxford and played a variety of sports as a child, excelling in cricket and rugby. She started playing rugby aged five and soon developed a reputation in her school as the player to be feared on the pitch. The main tactic of her team was to pass the ball to Maud, who would run through anybody in her way. She wore a bright pink scrum cap that would put the fear of God in the child it was headed towards. Maud now coaches one of the girls she played against as a child, and is happy to know that her reputation as 'the girl in the pink scrum hat' is still intact.

Alongside rugby was cricket. Maud played for Charlbury Cricket Club in Oxfordshire, and was described as the team's 'star batter' in her days with the team. Vicky Strode, who was her captain at Charlbury, told the *Telegraph* that there were certain attributes of Maud's cricket game that made it clear that her mind might have been on playing rugby. 'She was a force of nature in the way she played,' Vicky said. 'She would throw herself about and was never scared of getting hurt. It was almost like she'd dive if she didn't need to sometimes. It kind of makes sense with rugby.'

Maud played cricket mainly to please her mum, who loves the game and was less impressed with her daughter wanting to play the more aggressive sport of rugby. But as Maud's late teenage years approached, and with them the shortened attention span that comes with teenage life, she decided to focus on rugby, for Oxford Harlequins with the boys' team, then with a girls' team at the Gosford All Blacks, before representing the South West of England. Soon picked up by Wasps, a Premiership Women's Rugby team based in London, the aspiring player juggled training with Wasps in their centre of excellence alongside her A levels in geography, PE and psychology. On days she had training, by coaches including former Red Rose Danielle Waterman, Maud would leave sixth form to start the two-and-a-half-hour journey to Wasps' training ground, Twyford Avenue, in West London. She would get the train or a coach from Oxford to London, and cycle the rest of the journey out to the training ground. After training with Wasps, and then cycling to the train station and returning home to Oxford, it was time to get ready to go to school again the next day.

It wasn't long before Giselle Mather, a former England

star and the director of rugby at Wasps at the time, recognised the prop's talent and invited her to train with the senior squad. Reflecting on those days now, Maud believes the gruelling days of combining sixth form with playing at Wasps set her up for being a Red Rose. They were a test of her dedication, mental resilience and ability to perform under pressure. Every inch of her perseverance was tested. As with all challenges Maud faces, she rose to the occasion. She finished sixth form with grades of AAB, significantly higher than the Cs she had been predicted, and she was rewarded with a sports scholarship at Brunel University, which she gladly accepted. Not only was it a fantastic university offer, but it also drastically cut down her commuting time to Wasps.

Those long days are also part of what makes her one of the most dynamic props in rugby. As Maud was under 18, she was not allowed to play in her favoured position of the front row at Wasps, so she was forced to play in the second row – a position that tends to involve more running and passing. It developed her rugby skill set at a young age and forced her to be adaptable.

She was 18 when the coronavirus pandemic kicked in and women's rugby shut down for seven months. The Premiership Women's Rugby returned in October 2020, when Maud was 19 years old, and with its return came new law variations to reduce the amount of face-to-face contact. There were fewer scrums and lineouts and games were reduced to 70 minutes rather than 80.

It meant players had to adapt their game and the result was a more well-rounded crop of front-row specialists, with Maud leading the way. Fewer scrums meant fewer chances for players to catch their breath, and for forwards, they saved valuable energy from not having to form a scrum or lift in a lineout so often. 'There is more ball in play time in 70 minutes than there was in the 80 minutes of the normal laws,' Giselle told *The Times* in 2021. 'And the ball moves. You have to play. All my players now are fantastic handlers of the ball. As an unintended consequence it has been phenomenal.

'Last weekend, one of my tight-head props, Maud Muir, caught a high ball over her head, handed somebody off, charged down the wing, smashed someone out of the way and then did the most outrageous offload to Abby Dow.'

Maud soon became a starter in the Wasps Ladies (later renamed Wasps Women) side, again juggling playing in the Premiership Women's Rugby with studying for her degree, but caught the eye of rugby fans for her ferocious style. When she scored a hat-trick of tries against Sale Sharks in her breakthrough season in 2020–21, video clips of her playing went viral on social media and rugby fans were keen to see more of the rising star.

Ahead of the 2021 Six Nations, Maud was called up as a development player and got the chance to go into the senior England camp for the first time, gaining valuable coaching from the England staff as well as the chance to learn from more experienced front-row specialists such as Vickii Cornborough, Amy Cokayne and Lark Davies. Maud was named as a non-playing reserve in the opening two Six Nations games against Scotland and Italy, which gave her an insight into a match day as a Red Rose.

She made her debut against New Zealand in the autumn of 2021, in a record-breaking win against the team that would host the Rugby World Cup the following year. These autumn matches were a crucial test for Simon to trial his squad and rotate his selections to give up-and-coming players like Maud the chance to show their potential. Maud then played against the USA as part of a squad full of development players. Asked after the USA match if the autumn matches had helped him with his World Cup selection headaches, Simon had one player on his mind. 'Look at Maud Muir and what she's capable of doing,' he told the media after the match. 'She's put herself right in the frame for getting on the plane to New Zealand, from pretty much nowhere.'

As Maud sat in the meeting room listening to Simon explain the dedication needed to play in the World Cup, she was aware that her ability to play across the front row, and the dynamic style of her play, is both her strongest quality and a major factor holding her back from the starting line-up, as her utility makes her particularly valuable as a replacement option. It's a great position to be in, but everyone wants a starting shirt in a World Cup final. Maud had to use these training camps to prove that she could keep up with those who had been playing rugby before she was born and challenge them for their shirt.

Away from rugby, the young player is a social butterfly. She is happiest when surrounded by her friends. The prop spends hours snapping photos with her tight-knit friendship group and filming videos to look back on. Memories and friends are important to her and becoming a more prominent member of the England squad has brought her out of her shell. She fits in well as a buffer to some of the more assertive players in the squad and is liked by all. She does not cause friction and has earned the respect of team-mates for her bravery on the pitch.

Emily Scarratt

Emily Scarratt has been a Red Rose since she was 18 years old. The experience she has amassed playing for England since 2008, her entire adult life, means she is a natural leader in the squad. Emily is one of the most important members of the team, and behind the captain, she is the first name on the team sheet. She is quiet, wise and hugely respected by team-mates and opponents. Emily is the classic Red Rose: a professional to her core and world class at her best.

That dedication to her craft has made her one of the most successful rugby players in England's history. She is England's highest points scorer, in part due to the longevity of her career in which she has won the World Cup, in 2014, eight Six Nations titles, and her services to rugby were rewarded with an MBE, fittingly presented by Queen Elizabeth II. But these are moments of gold that flicker between recurrent injuries, heartbreaking losses and years painstakingly perfecting her talent.

As a toddler, Emily watched her brother play rugby and she first had a go at playing aged five, at Leicester Forest Rugby Club, where she played in a mixed-gender team until she was 12 years old. The RFU rules that from the under-13s team and upwards, girls can no longer play in the boys' team, but luckily for Emily her club was joining forces with Anstey RFC, and she could continue playing rugby union, but it still wasn't her main focus. As a child, Emily played a different sport on every night of the week.

She remembers representing her school in a netball fixture on a Monday during school hours, then playing basketball for her club that evening, and Wednesdays were often spent playing badminton for her school and then tennis at her local club in the evening. She also played hockey, cricket and rounders, but it was basketball that first offered her a taste of elite sport.

Emily is tall – 5ft 11¼in. tall, to be exact – which helped her in basketball. As a teenager, she would play a weekend fixture in the girls' team and a midweek fixture for the senior ladies' team. Aged 16, she was given the chance to go on a tour to the East Coast of America, the heartland of basketball, and toured New York, Washington, Philadelphia and Baltimore. When she arrived home, she got a letter in the post asking her to join an elite basketball programme at Manhattan College. She didn't take it seriously – to the point she cannot even remember if it was definitely Manhattan College that offered her a place – because by that time, rugby was her passion.

Emily moved to Lichfield Ladies, once a prominent team in the Women's Premiership, knowing she would play for the senior side once she turned 18. She was training with the girls' team and the senior women's team, although she was not allowed to do contact training with the adults.

She soon caught the eye of Gary Street, and she was called up to England. He remembers people saying the new prospect wasn't ready to play for England at such a young age and fielding concerns that she would not be confident enough to handle the pressure. As Gary presented Emily with her first England shirt, in the team's shirt presentation ceremony, those doubts were swept from his mind as she received the shirt with a wink at Gary. He couldn't believe his eyes. Fifteen years later, he chuckles at the thought of young Emily winking at him. 'Not confident? Hah!' Gary recalls thinking at the time, shaking his head. 'Scaz might have been young, but she was absolutely ready for that first cap.' And her confidence proved fair, as she is now the highest points scorer in England Rugby history and a World Rugby Player of the Year in 2019.

Emily – who is also known as Scaz, Scazzie and Scazidas among other nicknames – is a perfectionist. As the most experienced kicker in the squad, there is huge pressure on her shoulders, and taking an extra 30 minutes to practise her kicking helps ease some of the nerves. Everything on the rugby pitch is done in groups, almost like little sub-teams, including the scrum, the lineout and the backs. Everything in rugby is about teamwork, except for kicking. It's the one moment of silence and calm on a rugby pitch usually filled with the sounds of the crowd, the grunts of rugby players, or the screams of players asking for the ball. When kickers take a conversion or a penalty, signs light up the stadium that ask the crowd to respect the kicker. In general, the request is met with almost complete silence.

On the training ground, kicking with no distractions is a chance for Emily to reset and process the day gone by. The process of setting up a kick, stepping back, looking up at the posts and lining up her boot to the ball is a routine she has been perfecting since she began playing rugby aged five.

When England score a try, her process of taking a conversion remains the same every time. 'I go back and find what I felt was an appropriate distance to kick from, and being completely honest, we could score five tries in the same spot, and I might take it slightly back each time or closer each time,' she says. 'It just depends on what feels right. Then I find a spot to put my [kicking] tee down and I just kind of knock it into the ground a little bit until I am happy it is stable. Then I get the ball and I put the valve always facing towards the goal so you're kicking the opposite side of the ball, and I pop it on the tee.

'I put it on straight and then I give it a kind of a tilt to the right and then a tilt forward. So it's on a bit of an angle when it kind of sits on the tee. It looks a bit wonky really, but that's just how I keep the ball. It kind of opens up a little bit of that sweet spot for me. And then I would take my steps. It's back . . . wait, what do I do?' Emily pauses and giggles. She has done this routine so many thousands of times that it's just muscle memory for her now. 'It's hard to actually think about it because I just do it.' Emily pauses again as if she is replaying the move in her brain.

'My plant foot [the foot that stays next to the ball and isn't kicking] goes alongside the ball, and I take three steps back and two across, so you end up at a 45-degree angle to the ball. Then I do a few little taps of my kicking foot in the ground. There's no rhyme or reason to that, but it feels like you're pushing your toes to the end of your boot, which then makes you feel tighter and more in control of your boot, so you feel like you get a better connection. There's probably zero science for that but it's just a mental thing, I suppose.

'I have a few looks at the post, take a few deep breaths, and depending on how my kicking has been going, I might have one or two things in my head that I want to focus on. So sometimes that might be a strong left side, it might be getting through the ball, it might be just really focusing on the area of the ball that I'm trying to kick.'

The familiarity of the routine allows her to have a calm few minutes after the intensity of a Red Roses training session. These kicking sessions keep her on top of her game. The 1 per cent differences are what keep England at the top of the world rankings and keep Emily as the number one kicker in the world. There is something to be learned from every kick and Emily usually knows if it will be successful as soon as the ball leaves her foot. The relationship between her boot and the ball is like that of a snooker player and their cue. As the women's game gets more competitive, kicking success rate is becoming all the more important and hitting the ball only millimetres from the right spot can now be the difference between winning and losing a game. At the 2021 Rugby World Cup, a penalty kick by Wales scrum half Keira Bevan, in the dying moments of their Pool A match against Scotland, won them the game 18–15. That one successful kick secured Wales's chance to proceed to the quarter-finals.

Next is the mental preparation and trying to dampen the sounds of the stadium. 'It is almost like being underwater. You're in a swimming pool and it's really noisy, and then you kind of go underwater, and you know it's still noisy, but it's just completely muffled. I try to create that eerie silence in my head. In training it's a lot easier, because generally there isn't a huge amount of noise. But obviously in games it can be quite noisy, especially when you're playing away where people don't want to be quiet. Then when I'm ready, I take half a step backwards, and then go and approach the ball. Then I just hope for the best.'

She is a key member of the Thorns, a group of the most experienced Red Roses who lead on the off-pitch side of camp life, from the laundry to nutrition. A crucial part of that role is upholding the standards of behaviour and culture. Whether it's a quiet word in the ear of a player or a trusted chat with a coach, Emily is one of the wisest heads in the camp.

Jess Breach

Jess Breach is the modern Red Rose. She is the epitome of the age-grade systems and pathways working perfectly to produce an England player who can lift her team to greater heights. She is one of the fastest players in the team and one of the hardest to tackle.

Jess began playing rugby aged six at Chichester Rugby Club. She had watched her dad and her brother play and was offered the chance to join the boys' team. Soon, she was given the nickname 'The Jess Express', thanks to the speedy winger's ability to sprint down a touchline to score a try.

As a teenager, Jess was a promising athlete and hurdler, established in the national ranks as a prospect for the future. There was one problem, though; Jess loved rugby. 'Athletics helped rugby, but rugby didn't help athletics,' she says.

At the under-18 level in rugby, she was part of the Talented Athlete Sponsorship Scheme, a Sport England funded programme that helps get the best out of talented athletes and directs them towards the best opportunities. At the same time, Jess was moving up in the athletics sphere and was on the cusp of its under-20s programme too.

Jess would go to athletics meets and found the atmosphere

competitive and sometimes unfriendly. She remembers turning up and being asked lots of questions from her competitors about what her personal best was that season, what times she had been running, and how well she had been performing. There were no friends because the girls were all competing with each other and Jess felt as if nobody really cared for her. In sharp comparison, her rugby team was an incredibly supportive place where she got to train and play with her best friends. To Jess, that was what sport was all about. She would often turn up to athletics training with knocks or bruises from rugby and couldn't always take part in the full training sessions due to those rugby injuries. Her athletics coach told her that she had to make the choice between athletics or rugby, and at that point the choice was clear for Jess: rugby brought her the most joy, so she chose to follow what made her happiest.

In both 2014 and 2015 Jess won the European Sevens Grand Prix Series with England under-18s and captained the talent development group side in their match against Canada. In 2016, aged just 18, the rising star joined Harlequins and won the league and cup double that season. In 2018, before getting her debut for England, Jess played at the 2018 Sevens Rugby World Cup and was part of the bronze medal-winning team at the Gold Coast Commonwealth Games in the same year.

At 21 years old, she became one of the first 28 women to be given a full-time professional contract for England and in the same year she topped the try-scoring charts for the Women's Six Nations with a total of nine tries.

Despite her success, Jess is surprisingly uncompetitive. Even now, as one of the most exciting players in England's back line, she hates nothing more than the coaches suggesting a race because she detests going up against her friends. She feels a pressure because she is known for her speed, and doesn't like that others enjoy the challenge of trying to beat her. Rugby is fun for Jess. Nothing illustrates that better than how she remembers her debut for England. Her memories of what made it so special are all about sharing her debut with Zoe Harrison, her best friend, Ellie Kildunne and Hannah Botterman. She makes no mention of becoming the first person, man or woman, to score six tries on their debut. When that's put to her, she says one try felt particularly special: the one which Zoe set up for her.

Jess made a pact with Zoe, Ellie and Hannah to all get matching tattoos to commemorate the occasion, but she was the only one to go through with it. Not to let it happen again, she made her team-mates sign a contract to agree to get matching tattoos if they won the 2021 Rugby World Cup. The contract – via the notes app on Jess's phone – reads: 'Sarah Beckett and Zoe Harrison (added on 14 February 2022) are getting a tattoo if we win the World Cup in New Zealand with Jess. This was decided on Monday, the second of December 2021, time being 10.30 p.m.' Sarah Bern was added to the contract on 6 August, and Hannah Botterman was added on 22 August, and they agreed that the tattoo would be a small kiwi. Jess was taking no chances this time of her friends bailing on her and the contract, albeit a bit of fun, summarises Jess well. She is professional and takes her job incredibly seriously.

Jess was a fan of the Red Roses before she was one herself and went to watch them at three World Cups – 2010, 2014 and 2017. Her idol was Danielle Waterman, known as

'Nolli', the electric England full back with a skill set beyond her generation, and Jess got to play with Nolli before her international retirement in 2018.

After six tries on her first cap, Jess then scored five more tries on her second and brought new attention to the England women's rugby team as clips of her tries went viral.

She is close to her family, who travel the world to watch her play. Her dad was her rugby coach for years and while it tested their relationship at times after rows at training sessions, it has brought them closer together. Nobody quite understands this unique rugby journey like her dad. He wears a brightly coloured coat to her matches so she can spot him in the crowd and look at him whenever she gets the chance. He records every time Jess sings the national anthem, which she describes, in classic 'daughter describing her father' fashion, as 'so embarrassing'.

Jess comes from an incredibly supportive family, who travelled with her to two of the World Cups as women's rugby fans themselves and have been in the crowd for every match Jess has played for England. There was only one England match that her mum, Tricia, had to miss. While Jess was playing against France in an autumn fixture in 2019, Tricia was at home receiving treatment for cancer. It was so tough for Jess not to have her mum in the crowd that for once she didn't look for her dad when she sang the national anthem because of how much it would hurt her not to see her mum standing next to him. It was the one time that Jess was pleased her dad recorded her singing the anthem, so her mum could watch it from home. Tricia is in remission and Jess says the ordeal reminded her of how important family is to her.

Jess is marvellously switched on and aware that rugby does not last forever. She capitalised on the attention she received early in her career by signing commercial deals, and she always has one eye on the future. With a degree in sports marketing and communications from St Mary's University in Twickenham, plans to move into the media industry after retiring are already in place.

She is a key part of the first generation of Red Roses who have grown up in the game feeling valued and supported, not knowing the struggles of the amateur days that so many players contended with. Jess knows her worth because there has never been any doubt about the value she adds to the England rugby team.

Chapter 4

A HOLISTIC VISION OF SUCCESS

Life in an England camp is designed to provide players with the ultimate environment to perform at their best. 'Holistic' is the term the staff use; 'intense' is how the players describe it. The Red Roses spend a lot of time in camp, in preparation for major tournaments and for the duration of a competition like the Six Nations. Every last detail has been thought of: from who shares a room with whom to what food will be served at each mealtime. There is a team of men and women working in the background, keeping everything ticking and making sure that the players' only worries should be on their performances.

From the outside, it is easy to assume that the Red Roses have the perfect culture. They are the most supported team in women's rugby and the content shared on social media is always positive – but is camp life always so joyful? Of course not. No culture is perfect, and while the players in general report being happy and comfortable in the environment, the camps can be overwhelming and relationships can be tested.

The players do not have one base and instead travel around to different hotels throughout tournaments, whereas in comparison, the men tend to be based at Pennyhill Park in Surrey. The lack of consistency is difficult for players, and now they are used to high-performance environments at club level they feel less supported by England. 'We often talk about how Bristol Bears is the best programme around – I think it's a lot better than England's programme,' Abbie Ward says. 'I'm a better player at club [level] and I have a better set-up at club than I have at England. It's probably hard because England don't have a base, and I think that's probably one of the reasons. I used to feel like it would be pretty basic at club and then I would go to England, and that's where I would get my development, but it's the other way around, which is probably the same for the men too.'

Their busy schedules can be made tougher by how on top of each other the players can feel after a long time away from home. For weeks at a time and for 24 hours a day they are surrounded by their colleagues, eating all meals together and spending days off in each other's company. It can be intense, as Maud Muir says, and it can be difficult to make a strong culture when the team are only together for relatively short bursts of high intensity.

The players also essentially live with the coaches and staff for all of that time too, and both sides find that challenging. While the players and the staff are all England Rugby employees, the work environment is demanding and goes beyond the normal relationship people have with their colleagues. The players share bedrooms and eat all meals with their colleagues and bosses, so everyone sees each other's worst moments. While there are amazing times when players bond and relationships are strengthened, there can also be arguments, resentment and frustration that boil over.

The coaches have nearly always been men who are much older than the players and the team find it difficult to break down those generational barriers. 'I think the coach-player dynamic is unusual,' Maud Muir says. 'We're all England Rugby colleagues, and while the staff do need to be authoritative, I feel like we could be a lot more integrated. Even at mealtimes, players and staff are rarely integrated.'

Some members of staff, like Calum the analyst, do mix well with the squad, but it's the coaches in particular whom Maud would like to get to know better away from rugby. 'I would love to just have a little chinwag with the staff at mealtimes, that sort of thing. I don't want to feel constantly judged by the coaches in our down time, I want to feel relaxed in the periods when we don't have to think about rugby.'

Maud is on one end of the Red Roses spectrum as one of the younger players in the squad, but Emily Scarratt, who has been in the England set-up since 2008, agrees. 'Maud is right; those relationships [between coaches and players] are really important,' she says. 'Probably something we've perhaps not got quite right over the last few years is building better relationships between the players and the staff. A relationship is always stronger when you know someone better and I definitely think it's something that could be improved.'

It's a complex dynamic. The players, fully immersed in the all-encompassing environment, are surrounded every day by the same people who decide if they will play and who have tough conversations with them. They can feel watched and judged by the staff, even if that is not the staff's intention, and struggle to relax. While bonds are forged in moments of shared triumph, the strains of living and competing together can reveal cracks in the foundation of their culture. It's a hard relationship to nourish. There is a clear divide in how the players describe the culture to how the staff describe it. Players tend to talk more negatively about the relationships with the staff, whereas the staff only ever speak positively of the players. This will be in part because the players are more open with complaints than the staff, but also speaks of a discontent that some of the Red Roses feel.

'You can't really force culture,' Maud says. 'I'd love the culture to be like Gloucester-Hartpury or Wasps, but I just don't think that happens with international environments. We're not together long enough and there are so many different people from different teams that have different cultures. I just don't think international teams can be as close-knit as a club team; maybe I'm wrong, but that's what I've experienced so far.

'I love the Gloucester and Wasps environment and I think that's because of that family culture. There are snippets of that with England, but in the periods that we're together, we're only together in big intense blocks where people are competing against each other, which makes it difficult for a culture to flourish.'

Is the solution that players have their own social space that is just for them? I think I put the image of a 'No Staff Allowed' sign on the door in Maud's head. 'No, just in camp when we aren't training, I just want staff and players to be more integrated to ease the outside pressures and make the down-time environment more chilled. This can help us on the pitch as we have more trust in the coaching staff, so could improve our performances,' she says. 'It would be nice if coaches sat with us at mealtimes and we could just talk about normal life things.' The desire to connect on a personal level with the coaches, beyond the realm of rugby, simmers beneath the surface, offering glimpses of normality in a high-stakes setting, but the constraints of maintaining professional boundaries can hinder the natural flow of relationships, leaving some players yearning for deeper connections.

'It's a difficult situation as player-coach boundaries don't want to be crossed, so it's getting that balance right. I wouldn't have ever really sought out Midds [Simon Middleton] to have a casual conversation with him. Although Ellie [Kildunne] and I sat next to Midds on a meal out, and him and Ellie were talking about the North, and it was nice because it was normal. But those meals might happen every two or three weeks, whereas it could happen more often. I would like to know more about the staff's lives outside of rugby.'

The relationships are tricky for staff too, who have to navigate being the ones in charge. The camps have been compared to a boarding school before, although such a comparison infantilises the players and makes the staff sound stricter than they are. But it is a high-pressured environment where tempers often flare and emotions are close to the surface. Navigating good relationships is difficult for the players and the staff, and each player and staff member will report differently about how strong those relationships are.

'You've got to build relationships with players. I think connecting with the players is one of the biggest things I've learned since I have come in. I think you get more out of the players if you show them that you know them, and they know you,' Louis Deacon, the forwards coach, says.

'Communication is something to work on, definitely. I think in the [2021] World Cup there was a lot going on, for players and staff, and when we had down time we were trying to get away from the pressures of the tournament, so we probably didn't do enough together, not enough one-to-one time and things like that. So off the back of that, in the [2023] Six Nations, we were focused quite heavily on building that, and with Mitch [John Mitchell] in and moving forward, that's going to be a big part of our work.

'Initially I think it's about making the players know that you're available to talk. So we scheduled in slots where players could book in and have those conversations, but that's not the right way to do it. I think it needs to happen a bit more naturally than that. But off the back of those scheduled chats, it just began to happen more naturally.'

John Mitchell joined the Red Roses in the autumn of 2023, and Louis thinks the biggest learning curve for him will be how coaches should communicate with players. 'My biggest recommendation [to John] would be that, connecting and working on your communication side of things, when working with the Red Roses. On the pitch you need to give them the clarity around what you're asking them to do, giving them the detail within that, and then off the pitch players love a one-to-one feedback session. You've got to be approachable and get to know them and connect with them.'

The players and staff have all done work with sports psychologists to better understand their own personalities and communication preferences. Helen Davis, the team's sport psychologist from October 2021 to July 2023, helped the players to identify the colour profile of their personalities.

The players and staff completed questionnaires that identified which of the four personality colours they most closely
matched. To simplify the rather detailed psychology: Red
characters are bold, passionate and often angry. Yellow
people love being creative and happy. Blue people are
professional and trustworthy and green personalities are
perfectionists, analytical and inventive. Most people are a
mix of these colours. The team have worked on how each
colour likes to receive communication and also how they
talk to others, which has gone some way to helping players
and staff better understand each other, but little to resolve
issues of a breakdown in those relationships.

Simon's personality type is 'stereotypical red', Emily
Scarratt says, which is associated with more assertive people. 'That means he reacts quite quickly and his opinions
are quite strong. I do feel they are good characteristics of a
head coach because you don't want someone to be dither-
ing around with a decision or whatever. You need to have
answers pretty quickly.'

One of the pinnacles of the Red Roses' culture is respect
for all, and while no culture is ever 100 per cent foolproof,
that team culture is fundamental to the group's success. The
environment the team train and play in is demanding and
by the very nature of rugby being a team sport, there is no
room for egos in the side. The staff behind the team are
central to creating a space that not only gets the best out of
players but also creates the best people too.

There are a myriad of factors that contribute to the culture of the team, and while no culture is perfect, it starts
with having the right people in charge. As the support staff
and coaches have joined the team, it has been important

to Simon Middleton, the former head coach from 2015 to 2023, that they possess the good characteristics that make them an asset to the team.

To work for the Red Roses, you must be technically excellent at your role, whether that be on the coaching, logistics or medical side of things, but decisions on hiring personnel often come down to the type of people who will be good for the team's culture. The same goes for players, and there have been many times that players have not been picked in further tournaments because their attitudes and behaviour did not match England's culture.

'What you have to do first of all is to make sure you work with that player,' Simon says, when explaining how he deals with a player who is not suitable for the environment. 'They need to understand where they fit in terms of, "Yes, you're a great player, but these negative qualities that you are displaying are outweighing your ability." You can add by taking away sometimes, and I've certainly found that there are players who we have stayed away from a bit because they weren't quite the right fit for us, and those who we have stayed away from have been high maintenance within the squad. I've seen it a million times, where you have players who demand so much of the staff around you, and it becomes to the detriment of the rest of the squad. No player should dominate any member of staff's time.'

So what is the Red Roses' team culture? The crux of it is that no player is more important than another. 'The culture is one of huge expectations on how we perform, how we train, how we commit ourselves to going about our business and how we conduct ourselves,' Simon says. 'So it's an expectation that no one is better than anyone else.

'There's a way that we speak to each other. There's a way that we treat each other. And absolutely, there have been a lot of occasions where that's not been the case. But I think the fact that we built expectations and allowed players to have conversations with each other that said, "Hang on a minute, that's not acceptable. That's not how we go about what we do." Those conversations iron out a lot of issues. I'm sure there's lots of little issues that go on within the Roses that the players have ironed out themselves before I'm even aware of them because of the culture we've created. It's very much: "This is the expectation, this is how we behave." You only need to have a few of those conversations amongst the players to eliminate that type of stuff.'

An issue that the coaches report is arrogance from players who have moved up from the club game to England. It takes a while for some players to understand the team dynamic and culture at England, and some have to be reminded to behave in line with the international side's values. 'The players act very, very differently when they come into England from when they are with their clubs,' Simon says. 'We have a very specific way of how we train and behave and it's very different to what most players have in their clubs. You have a lot of players who come to us as very big fish in their clubs, they probably get away with an awful lot in their clubs, and certainly have a lot more say in how things are run in their clubs. That's not the case when it comes to England. They're just one more fish in the pond. And yes, they have a voice, everybody has a voice, but it all feeds into what we feel is the right direction for the team.'

Beneath the surface of this seemingly idyllic culture lies a nuanced reality, where the challenges of constant togetherness and the strain of competing against one another can test even the strongest relationships. The delicate balance of authority and camaraderie is an ongoing pursuit, with both sides striving to bridge the gaps and foster understanding. The bottom line, as always, is that they share the same purpose: everyone in the environment wants the Red Roses to be the number one team in the world. They might just have different ideas of how to get there.

The set-up of the England camp is fascinating. The team tends to stay in hotels, such as the Village Hotel in Bracknell, that have experience hosting sports teams. The hotel must have enough twin bedrooms to allow the players to share, two in each room, and enough space to allow the players their own private area to relax in during tournaments. As you walk into the hotel, there's little clue that the team are staying there. The only hints of the team's stay might be someone in England-branded clothing (or 'stash' as it is affectionately known) at the check-in desk or a player hidden in the corner of the hotel reception on FaceTime to a relative. As the door opens to the Red Roses private area, the room is full of England Rugby staff and players spread across tables and sofas. Everyone tends to be in England tracksuits, which are piled high on a table and labelled by size to make sure the players have all the kit they need. There are players in the meeting room to the right of the main room and some are being treated by the physiotherapists in the room to the left. There are conversations happening over coffee, players making smoothies, and some playing board games around a table.

The woman at the heart of managing the team and the environment is Harriet Martin. If the Red Roses are the boat cruising the ocean, the background staff are in the engine rooms, they are the servers, the power that keeps the ship afloat and gliding the seas. The captain of that ship is Harriet. 'Operations manager' is her official title, but a more realistic title would be 'team problem solver, chief organiser and mentor'.

Harriet describes her job as worrying about the details needed to get everyone where they need to be at the right time on the field of play, performing as they need to. One side of that is the logistics: the accommodation, the travel, the food, the kit, and the other side is being a conduit between the players and the staff. In that part of her role, she is the middlewoman who makes sure everyone is aligned. If they are not, she is there to make sure feedback is passed on to the right people. Sometimes she just needs to be a good listening ear for people to vent to.

It's a simplified explanation of one of the most demanding jobs in the set-up. Her work, in reality, stretches far beyond what any job description could offer. A good job done, in her words, is when she has anticipated what a player needs before they ask for it. She looks so deeply into all the details of the players' lives in camp that she knows what problems they will encounter and stops issues arising before they appear. This translates into everyday scenarios: taking an extra pair of undershorts for the player she knows is going to forget their own, packing sanitary wear and extra shorts for the players on their periods, and having countless hairbands in her pocket, equipped to respond to the inevitable calls of 'er . . . Harriet?' on a match day. Her job includes tasks like making sure all luggage being taken to the Rugby World Cup is checked in the day before by her, so players cannot lose their luggage or have to carry it around the airport, and organising who shares a room with whom. It's anticipating every problem the team may face and being one step ahead, always.

Harriet is thoughtful but stern on first impression. There is a sense of an exterior calmness, but behind her eyes are a million open brain tabs of the different things she is responsible for. It's an impression she is aware of and to illustrate her point she uses the example of a player asking her if they can all go out for dinner that evening. The player expects a simple answer of yes or no, but Harriet is considering what restaurant would take a booking of nearly 50 people (players and staff), how they would get there, if there are any schedule conflicts, and what is happening the following morning. Oh, and is James, the nutritionist, going to be OK with that? Did he have something else planned? And what would the cost implications be? What restaurant would all the players be happy with? What about dietary requirements? Should the players be in their Red Roses leisurewear or casual clothes? 'I'll get back to you,' she simply says. The player continues their day unaware of the logistical challenge they have posed. And the answer, by the way, was yes.

Harriet puts a lot of effort into looking calm, as she realises that if she looks stressed it could make the players feel stressed. She is like a duck paddling on water. On appearance, she is calm, cool and collected, but there is a constant to-do list that she is managing. It's marvellously impressive, and there should be no suggestion here that she is overwhelmed by her responsibilities. The opposite is true – this is the woman you want to organise your entire life.

There would be no missed doctor's appointment or birthday forgotten if Harriet was in charge of your day-to-day operations. I imagine her to be the friend who collects the passports at the start of a girls' holiday, books the airport transfer and knows if the hotel room has Wi-Fi before she has checked in herself.

Her meticulous attention to detail is quite something. She works with the coaches and plans the schedule so that every department's needs are met. So, if a coach says there will be a lineout session on one day, Harriet will factor in 20 minutes of strapping beforehand, and include it on the schedule. Her role in that sense is to make sure that the staff are all on the same page and happy with the week's plan.

The team travel a lot which can cause stress for Harriet, and there was no greater feat than the 2021 Rugby World Cup in New Zealand. Harriet did a lot of planning before the tournament, including doing a site visit out there to get an idea of the hotels and the area, and work out solutions to logistical challenges.

The team travels with a lot of kit and, because of regulations brought in after Brexit, Harriet has to write down every item of kit, its serial number and its value before travelling. Crucially, too, she has to make sure the plane is prepared to take the amount of equipment the team has. She will work out what time is best for the team to fly so that it's not too early or too late, which would risk upsetting their sleep schedules. She also considers how to make it as relaxing as possible and knows the players love to eat at the airport, so she will make sure there is time in the schedule for that too.

In these scenarios, it might come across that the players

are selfish or childlike, unable to fend for themselves, but that's not the case. They have such great pressure on their shoulders that small details like remembering to pack socks can easily be missed. They need Harriet to steer them in the right direction and allow them the focus of turning up and just being told what to do and where to be.

It's important to Harriet that the players are well-rounded people so she makes it clear that there are expectations on the team as well as the staff. They should drop off their own laundry and help pick up equipment at the end of training sessions, for example. They should keep their rooms and communal areas tidy and not expect anyone to pick up after them. As professionalism comes into the game, she wants the players to be polite and able to do things for themselves. 'You definitely notice the players that have had a job and come into the environment versus someone that comes straight into this environment,' she says. 'Performance is always the main focus, but you also want rounded people. As the game becomes professional, you don't want to produce players that demand everything. We want to give them the most they can to perform. But that doesn't mean they can't have basic life skills that we still want.'

The result of such a culture is players who, generally speaking, get on very well. Players will share rooms and while they get to choose whom they share with, sometimes the players are encouraged to share with new people in order to mix up the team. Some players always room together when they can: Zoe Harrison and Jess Breach, Alex Matthews and Marlie Packer, Emily Scarratt and Mo Hunt. Sometimes completely opposite characters are paired up, like Connie Powell and Tatyana Heard.

Whereas Connie gets her energy from other people and enjoys being in a group environment, Tatyana is much happier on her own. Her dream day is to have a coffee, get her nails done and read her book in uninterrupted peace. The pair get on really well and are friends despite their very opposite personality types. Connie thinks their dynamic works well because she goes and spends time with the group, while Tatyana stays in the room on her own. 'Tats', as she is known, knows she is always invited to spend time with the group, but it's just not what she wants to do. Some players are very different behind the closed door of their room, like Marlie. Her room-mate Alex says that while Marlie is a huge character during training and when with the group, she is softer and quieter when she is on her own. She is reflective and spends a lot of her time on the phone to her son Oliver, whom she misses a lot when she is in camp.

That suits Alex well, who is a quieter figure and likes to spend time on her own too. It's about finding a good balance and respecting each other, the players say, and that respect is even more important when the team are away for tournaments and spending a lot of time together. It's essentially having to share a bedroom with your colleague for up to 12 weeks, so the rule many players stick to is no work chat in the bedroom. Instead discussions tend to be about the TV shows they are watching, or what family members are doing at home. In camp, conversations around the massage beds, in the physio room and in the canteen tend to be about whichever show is the current favourite. *Married at First Sight* is a common choice, as is *EastEnders*. That's because Connie has made members of the team watch *EastEnders*, having never missed an episode herself. Some players, including Poppy Cleall, now loosely follow the soap and others have taken it a bit more seriously. Connie recently caught Sarah McKenna sneaking in ten minutes of an episode while waiting for a gym session to start.

As camps progress, the bar for what makes the players laugh gets lower and lower. 'We are institutionalised,' Poppy says, during the final week of a Six Nations camp, after belly-laughing with tears in her eyes at a comment made about an idea for a TV show called *Maud Abroad,* where the clumsy-but-lovable Maud would travel the world with cameras following her. At one point during a stretching session, the players got into a light-hearted but lively debate about whether they would brace for impact if they were on a plane that was crashing. The debates are common and can last for hours.

Away from the ground, this is a group of young women enjoying each other's company. They film dances for TikTok, laugh stupidly at mundane things. Many choose to spend their days off together. The players find humour and fun at every opportunity, but as soon as the players are training, they can easily flick the switch for work mode. Sarah Bern is perhaps the most ferocious example of this. Away from the pitch, she is a softly spoken and friendly person, yet on the training pitch it's as if someone invited a *Peaky Blinders* character to lead England's scrum. Her persona changes completely.

While camp life is full of random moments of fun, there is a lot of hard work to get done. Every day in a Red Roses camp is named after the day's purpose, helping the players set their intentions by creating a clear structure around each day.

Here is what a week looks like in a Red Roses camp as they prepare for a Test match on a Saturday:

Monday: Prime day

The first day of the week is used to prime the players for a Test-match week

Players have medical check-ups, followed by meetings between the leadership group, the scrum group and the lineout group among others. After lunch, the team has an upper body gym workout followed by an on-pitch walk-through of game situations, split between forwards and backs. Then the whole team jog through match situations for one hour. In the evening, there is dinner and a chance to check in with the physiotherapists as well as some player group meetings.

Tuesday: Battle day

The most physically demanding day of the week

This is the hardest day of the week. During breakfast there will be meetings to discuss things like strategy and lineouts, then the team travels to Pennyhill Park where they will do a lower body gym session before the backs and forwards are initially split to work on fundamental skills. The forwards will then do a scrum factory and lineout contests and the backs will work on kicking and handling skills. The team then travel to Bisham Abbey for lunch. After lunch is the main training session of the week, which includes technical aspects of the set piece and a full-contact short game. On Tuesday evenings, players are often allowed to go out for a healthy dinner and the team for the weekend is announced at 8 p.m.

Wednesday: Grow the gap

Players have a day to fill how they wish

The team have the day off and have a lot of time to spend how they like, but will be offered opportunities to improve off-pitch parts of their game. Soft tissue massage therapists come in, the team psychologist has drop-in sessions, and the players can check in with staff members like the physiotherapist or doctor. Most players use this down day to go for coffee, have naps and play board games.

Thursday: Race day

This day is all about speed and power

Players have a power session in the gym, filled with exercises like box jumps and fast lifts. This is to help prime the players to work on their speed and explosiveness in game situations. After lunch, the players have a team meeting where the coaches explain what they want to get out of the training session, before the players go on to the field. This session has drills based on increasing speed, and includes races to develop players' acceleration. There are also match-based scenarios that the players go through at full speed, including lineouts.

Friday: Captain's run

The final day of preparation

The players arrive at Twickenham to do their captain's run, led by captain Marlie Packer. This is the final chance to fix any issues and perfect the details of the game plan for the match. In the evening, the team tend to have more carbohydrates than usual to help prepare them for the match.

Saturday: Game day

What it all comes down to

The team have their last light meal about three hours before kick-off. They arrive at the stadium and have a warm-up session before going back into the changing rooms for a quick team talk and to get shirts on. Players are offered supplements like caffeinated chewing gum before they leave the tunnel.

Being a Red Rose comes with enormous mental pressure and the camps are often gruelling. England are billed as one of the most formidable teams in the world and have a target on their backs every time they play. To become a Red Rose, you must have the mental toughness to excel at elite rugby while managing the day-to-day pressures of real life. By the time the players join the camp, they are already high-performing tough women, many of whom have had to juggle their playing careers with work, university and the general stressors of everyday life. So the role of the team's sports psychologist is as much managing their wellbeing as it is helping them become the best athletes in the world.

'If you have high wellbeing, generally you're going to get high performance,' Helen, the former sports psychologist for the team, says, as we catch up in a camp before she left her role. 'If players are in a good place, they can expect to get the best performance, and if they are not in a good place, performance can be compromised.'

Helen doesn't separate performance psychology from wellbeing, because for her the two go hand in hand. Environments that support wellbeing are key enablers of performance, she says. There are times when Helen's focus is solely performance psychology, like when she leads group sessions about mental skills, or when she advises coaches on how they can use psychology to help the players perform best, but in general the players used Helen for wellbeing check-ins and being a good listening ear.

Helen is around the camp at all times and has little chats with players as they go about their day. When she first started with England, in the lead-up to the 2021 Rugby World Cup, she became the team's unofficial water carrier during training sessions so that she could get a glimpse of the players in their high-stress environment. There are drop-in psychology sessions available to players, but they can also text Helen at any point and she will go and see them. 'I've spoken to players at half-past nine, ten o'clock at night, and the early mornings,' she says. 'They just know that I'm available at any time and they can send me a WhatsApp message saying, "Are you free?", or they can come up to me and ask me for a quick word; it doesn't really matter where we are. I would say some of the best conversations I have with players are what I call micro-conversations, when you're in the corridor, in the lift, or you're walking back to the coach. Because I'm in the environment all the time, it's not confined to those drop-in sessions. If I actually see something on the pitch or in a training session, I clock it and make sure to catch up with that player later.'

Because Helen was around the players so much, she has become aware of the players who would happily sit and chat to her, and the players who would actually find it difficult to sit down and discuss how they are feeling with her. With those players, Helen would just try to catch a passing moment at dinner and remind them that she is available if they want to talk. Often, that is enough.

Helen's background is in primary school teaching, a career that spanned 25 years, but her passion has always been psychology and her degree was in the same subject. She joined teaching with the idea of becoming an educational psychologist, but having worked with one as a teacher she decided it wasn't for her. In those 25 years Helen moved to Boston in the United States and for a while managed a programme where volunteers from the corporate world would use their lunch break to read to children who were not being read to at home, but it was when she moved back to England that she decided to step away from teaching for good.

Helen has always been a swimmer and was inspired by two swimmers at her club to pursue sports psychology. 'I was swimming and training with Cambridge Triathlon Club. Two of the women in the club were in the top ten in the world, and we would do the training sessions together and then go for brunch,' Helen says. 'I just listened to them talk about their careers in triathlon and it was really interesting listening to their psychology. Swimming was the weakest discipline for both of them and I remember saying: "It's almost like you get on the bike and your race is beginning, but what about the swimming? Just imagine if your mindset was stronger around the swim – it might change how you swim."

'I got a bit more curious about it, then I started Googling and I discovered that there was a Master's degree in sport and exercise psychology, which there wasn't when I did my degree, and I discovered it was a relatively new field. Aged about 43, I signed myself up to do this distance learning Master's while my three children were all going through exams at the same time.'

Since then, Helen has been one of the lead sports psychologists for Swim England, has worked extensively with Commonwealth, European and World Champions, and Olympic and Paralympic medallists from a wide range of sports. Helen has also worked with Cambridge University's women's rowing team as they prepared for The Boat Race. The latter is a particularly interesting part of Helen's CV. Her role as sports psychologist was to help the rowers prepare for one race which would determine whether their years of preparation, study and intense training would be rewarded with them being a winner or a loser, and the winning margin is often incredibly small. 'They were unbelievable,' Helen recalls of the squad she worked with. 'The hours they put in, to do lectures from nine to five, and then do intense training. At that point I had never worked with such a curious, highly intelligent, motivated group of people. They were incredible.'

What is particularly interesting in the context of Helen's work with the Red Roses is how she helped them manage the challenge of balancing their education with the training. As Helen explains this, in a meeting room in the England team's base during the Six Nations, sitting behind her is a table of players completing university assignments. Helena Rowland and Ellie Kildunne had assignments due that week and had to balance the intensity of a training camp with completing their coursework. Despite rowing being such a different sport to rugby, the lessons Helen learned there have been valuable for the Red Roses.

In preparation for the World Cup, she spoke to the squad and found their most common concern was a fear of being away from home for so long and spending so much time in camp with players and staff. So Helen had the idea of a Wellness Action Plan for each player. She stood in front of the Red Roses and said, 'Wellness Action Plan is a bit of a mouthful, we'll call them WAPs for short.' The team fell on the floor laughing and Helen wasn't sure why. Reader, if you are not aware of the pop culture reference here, and what a WAP is, I'm afraid I am not allowed to write it. Google at your own discretion (and if you are under 18, please do not Google it, but just trust me that it means something rude). Poor Helen stood innocently at the front of the room, ready to talk about the team's wellbeing, as the team were in a fit of giggles having been told they would each have their own WAP. The joke was explained to the older or more innocent members of the team who also did not know what WAP means. A group of players approached Helen and said, 'Look, we're not being rude and we're not laughing at you, but do you know what that means?' Helen was quickly given a short education about WAPs, and suggested a name change to save the giggles at every mention of WAPs, but the players decided it was too funny to change.

So WAPs became an integral part of preparing the team mentally for the World Cup. Helen did an individual plan for each player before World Cup selection, finding out the individual concerns of each player. There were common concerns such as selection and feeling homesick, and Helen worked with them to consider what had worked last time that player had been away from home for a long period of time, or what things didn't help that they would like to do less of. Every player is different, and some players wanted to chat to family members every day of the tournament whereas others said they felt happier when they were not in constant communication with home, because it made them miss their loved ones even more. Each player devised a plan for how they would keep in touch with family and friends at home. One player made a group chat so she could share her photos and feelings in one place and not have to text lots of different people with the same messages, for example.

Those chats with Helen also gave players a chance to share if there was anything going on at home that might affect their mood or performance while in New Zealand. Players could share as much or as little as they wanted to about anything that might prove a distraction, including relationship issues or family members being ill. A key discussion was how they would want to be informed if there was bad news from home. Helen asked who the player's support person would be, maybe a close friend in the camp, a family member who would be travelling to New Zealand, or maybe someone back home.

The plans would be followed by Helen and any other member of staff necessary. Midway through the tournament, the players' plans were reviewed to see what had been working and what hadn't. What many players found is that there were things they hadn't anticipated struggling with, such as feeling socially drained from so much time spent together, and other things that they were coping with better than expected.

The conversations are confidential but Helen's role is to support the team, which sometimes means sharing concerns with the coaches. Players will always be aware if that is going to happen. 'Those wellness action plans were confidential in my eyes,' Helen says. 'If there's anything that I think is important to report back to the coaches, I would talk to a player prior to that. They might say to me, "I don't want you to say anything," but if I was concerned from a performance aspect or anything like that, I would have a conversation with the player and say that it might be a good idea if they mentioned it to the coaches. So, it can be confidential, and I'll use my professional judgement on what's appropriate or not. What I generally did, and I shared this with the players first, is give back general comments to the coaching team and the staff. So explaining in general terms what players' main concerns were, or generally speaking, the things that a lot of people have said would help them when they're away.

'If a player has been particularly upset or has offloaded something to me, I'll ask them if they want me to make the coaches aware, and then I talk to the coaches. I might say that a player has something going on at home and I'm not going to divulge what that might be, but if they are off today don't read too much into it. Sometimes players have said they are happy for me to share some news with the staff, a break-up or something like that, because they worry that if they are not feeling 100 per cent it may translate into a training session and they don't want the coaches to think they are playing badly. But I've never been in a situation [with England] where I have had a real concern and have had to break confidentiality and share something with the coaches that the player doesn't want me to share.'

Some players say they were suspicious of Helen when she first joined the team, unsure of her role in selection decisions, and uneasy about feeling watched by someone who might be psychologically evaluating them at all times. For many that feeling lasted until Helen left the team in July 2023. Helen did a lot of work with the players on understanding her role, and finds that a good way to break down those barriers is by relaxing with the players. 'Relationships are the key to everything,' she says. 'I'm aware that I'm a staff member, I'm a person who forms that connection between coaches and players and other staff members and players. It's a delicate balance. I'm not their age, I'm not sitting around talking to them about the latest whatever, because that's not my role. But I love sitting down with them and playing a game with them, or doing a sing-song when I can join in. I don't want to be there all the time because they like to just do their own thing as well, so it's just about that balance.'

A big challenge Helen found is that the players are not as accustomed to sports psychology as she expected them to be. 'It's been a very big learning curve for me,' she says. 'I think one of the main reasons for that is I have come into an environment that has had very mixed sports psychology experiences with various different people. It's been mixed, I would say. When you come into a new job we all have ideas and I had to really learn what the environment was that I was coming into and how psychology is perceived.

'Considering it's a national team, they've not had a consistent approach with it and I guess I thought they would have more experience of psychology. I think there's very differing opinions about where they see psychology sitting [in the programme]. My approach has very much been that I'm not going to force myself on anybody, and it's about building relationships with people and letting them know I am available, should they wish to talk to me. But, and this is where I think it's still an ongoing piece of work for me, this environment is a reactive environment, and it doesn't need to be. I would love to see a really proactive environment where there is an ongoing curiosity about themselves and how psychology influences and improves performances.'

Helen sat on the Thorns group, the strategy group, and joins in on all the forwards and backs meetings so that she can get a well-rounded picture of what the players are facing. Once a week, Helen sat down with the medical team, including the team doctor and physiotherapists, to look holistically at the players and talk through any issues they might be having. 'Sometimes one of the physios might say that someone was down when they came into [the] physio [room], and we just talk about the players generally to make sure we are all aware of what is going on.'

Helen worked with, and through, the coaches as well as the players. Before and after the World Cup she met with Louis Deacon, the forwards coach, and Scott Bemand, the attacks coach, to talk about how they deliver training sessions, and helped them communicate well with players. Helen set the coaches some targets and did some observations to help them work on the day-to-day conversations with players, which proved helpful especially as the team were in big match weeks and emotions were high.

Helen's most interesting project before the World Cup

was around selection. As chapter six will explore in more detail, not being selected for a major tournament can be absolutely heartbreaking for players. 'Midds [Simon Middleton] spoke to me about selection because he recognised it was such a massive issue,' Helen says. 'I went away and thought about how I could talk to players about selection. Players do not like evening meetings and they don't want to sit through a psychology lecture. So a big challenge for me was to bring psychology to life in a way that's a bit creative. So I recorded some conversations with players about their feelings towards selection, how they dealt with the pressures of it, maybe stories about selection in the past, and I asked the coaches for their stories about when they weren't selected as players.

'I also asked the coaches what it is like to deliver that news, because I wanted the players to recognise that actually it's really difficult for the coaches as well. So I pieced together, having never done anything like this before, a series of four audios, where we had player and coach comments interspersed with some psychological coping skills for managing selection. So it got the psychology in there, but also I was hoping it was a bit more interesting and captivating because the players were sharing how they felt. And most of the feedback I had from it was just that it was nice to hear from other people that they go through the same worries and concerns about selection, because they don't often talk about how they really feel about things.

'But also hearing from coaches, they had some pretty massive blows in their playing careers with selection so I think hearing that helped players as well.'

During the World Cup, Helen engaged all players and

staff in creating a charter called 'Be a Red Rose' which summarised the values they felt would enable everyone to feel a part of the World Cup, no matter what their role was. The players discussed the verbal and non-verbal behaviours and actions of Red Roses, to produce a charter where everyone felt valued in their role, whether they were a starter, finisher or non-playing reserve.

Those values, plus highlights from past successes and match memories from the previous 12 months, were collated and presented on an enormous visual timeline display on a wall of the hotel during the World Cup final week. The aim was to remind players of how they felt during previous successful matches prior to the World Cup, to think how those memories enhanced their performance, and to instil confidence for what was ahead. This charter continued into the 2023 Six Nations tournament.

Preparing players mentally for the strain of a tournament is just one part of a wide picture. To prepare players' bodies, there are physiotherapists, a doctor, a strength and conditioning team and a nutritionist.

To fuel players' performances, they must eat the right food. Nutrition is an increasingly important part of the high-performance environment and Dr James Morehen, the team's nutritionist, has worked closely with the players and staff to create a better culture around nutrition.

'My understanding in the women's game is that we're trying to drive an elite level set-up of high performance,' James says. 'So if you look at any high-performance team in the world, one thing that they will all have is a chef that travels with the team, and they'll have a full-time nutrition set-up, because we know how important food is. To think of an analogy, you're not going to run a Formula One car off crude oil, you're putting the best quality petrol in that car so that it can do what it needs to do.'

On a day-to-day basis in camps, players have a buffet for breakfast, lunch and dinner and they are educated well about what foods to go for, how much to eat, and when to eat what food. The menus are prescribed by James, who works with the hotels or training bases to make sure they are providing high-quality food, but the players are able to load their plates with the food they want to eat.

James looks at the schedule from Harriet and chats to the strength and conditioning team and the coaches to see how intense the training will be. He will then tailor the food diaries to the specific needs of that day. So travel days will be light on carbohydrates, and players will eat a high amount of carbs on training days. On those days, James will also add recovery foods and anti-inflammatories and antioxidants to the menu to help the players recover.

'A really good anti-inflammatory food would be oily fish, like salmon,' James explains. 'So you've got the omega-3, omega-6. What you wouldn't want on a day where they are smashing the crap out of each other [in training] is fried chicken, because it's inflammatory, which is not going to help them recover from that session.' Mixed berries are available at all mealtimes because they are a really good antioxidant food, which can help with inflammation and soreness.

As much effort as James puts into the menu, the execution of the cooking is in the hands of the chefs and kitchen staff at whichever base England are in. As of the 2023 Six Nations, the team did not have a full-time chef, but this is something the RFU are hoping to introduce ahead of the 2025 Rugby World Cup.

This hasn't always gone to plan, and James is often frustrated when food is presented poorly or the chefs do not stick to the menu. Kitchens that are not used to catering for athletes often add things like chips to a menu. While no food is banned in a Red Roses camp, deep-fried food can be inflammatory and so it is not encouraged. There was one incident in the 2023 Six Nations camp when the chefs put curly fries out, much to the players delight, and James had to walk around and encourage every player to consider healthier carbs.

'Because we move hotels a lot, we don't have that base with England, so it's harder to know what kind of quality the food will be,' Sarah Bern says. 'If we're in a new hotel every week, James has to speak to the chef and then the first time the food comes out, it could be chicken nuggets and wedges. And then Robin [Eager, the women's athletic performance manager] is running around shouting, "Don't eat the chips! Don't eat the chips!" and then the next day, it'll be a salad bar, there will be salmon and different options. I think it's more challenging because we move a lot. Whereas if we had a chef or we had a base, we would know exactly what we were getting. It would be a lot smoother and a lot easier.'

James is hoping that the team will have both a full-time base and chef soon. 'The success of the delivery of that menu, unfortunately, isn't on me, it's the chef,' James says. 'And it's where it's a real struggle sometimes with the Roses because we don't have a chef. So the success of that delivery comes down to the passion and the knowledge and the education of the chef.

'The men [England's men's senior rugby team] have a chef. As I understand it, he has a full-time job, but when England are training they basically take him out of his full-time job and he becomes their chef. And what's really good is the chef builds rapport with the players. He understands what each player likes, and he also understands what a rugby menu should look like when it's been delivered.

'So the problem that I have is that I can write the best menu in the world and send it to a hotel with loads of pictures and say this is how I want it delivered and presented, but if they are not passionate about women's rugby, then they're not going to be that bothered about how it looks. And by the way you see this in the men's game as well,' James, who is also the nutritionist at Bristol Bears, says. 'It's almost rolling the dice. Sometimes the food is amazing – we had great meals in Cardiff, for example, because the kitchen was used to preparing menus for rugby players.'

Presentation is really important to James. He loves food and wants mealtimes in camps to be enjoyable, not restrictive, environments. 'When you go to a restaurant, if the ambience is amazing and the food's amazing, you've had a great evening. But if you go to a hotel, it could be the nicest hotel in the world, but if the food's crap you give it a bad review.'

Food is a hot topic in camp and there is a clear psychological advantage to the players enjoying the food they are eating. As I chat to players in the camp about their food, they speak of a crumble and ice cream they had for dessert with the adoration of an *I'm a Celebrity . . . Get Me Out of Here* campmate talking about the one sweet they win in a challenge.

'Food for players in camp is such a big win,' James says. 'It is so important we get it right. A great example is that players told us they often have bacon medallions the day before games, and in this camp we hadn't put bacon on because I've been a little bit wary about the quality of the meat. But we put it on and what happened was all the girls loved it, they were so excited. So I could directly impact the psychological side of a player's game as well as the physical side of it.

'Food is so much more than energy. Food is family, food is religion, food is social. I quite often say that everybody in the world eats so everyone's entitled to an opinion on food, but what I will educate them on is what performance nutrition looks like. So am I going to tell Marlie Packer that she can't have a slice of birthday cake with her son? No, of course not, but I will say to her maybe don't have it the night before a game, because it might upset your stomach.'

There's a fine balance to be found for James in getting the best food in the players and supporting them to reach their goals, but also making sure no player is creating unhealthy eating habits. The players are in an ultra-competitive environment and so James makes sure the players are educated enough to understand the need to fuel their bodies appropriately and the benefits of eating well. For James, nutrition should be about creating a healthy relationship with food.

'The key thing for me as a nutritionist, especially as a bloke, is to build a level of trust with the players. For me to sit down with a woman and start talking about weight and food, what I have to do as early as possible is build that relationship. What I try to say to all the girls is that I don't really care what the number on the scale says. What I'm bothered about is if they are healthy, and how I can support them to be the best player in the world.

'Now, if that means that we look at dropping a little bit of weight, I will help them do that. If it means actually we look at putting on a bit of weight, I'll help them do that. So Ellie Kildunne has been a great example. She is probably the heaviest she's ever been but she's also the quickest she's ever been.

'Jess Breach was in a similar situation where she was really concerned about hitting a higher number on the scale, because she had never been there before. I said to her, "Well, Jess, if that two kilogram gain in weight is muscle mass, and you're quicker, and you're stronger, surely that makes you a better player?" and that tends to help shift the focus. What I try and get across to the girls is that it's not all about the number on the scale. It's how high are you jumping in the gym? How strong are you in the gym? How quick are you on the GPS? And can you last 80 minutes of international rugby? And if you can, I'm not bothered whether you're 65 or you're 75.

'I said to Jess: "If I put you on a scale, but I blindfold you from the number, so you don't know what a number says, we then go away and we have four weeks where me, you and Robin work on you. I help you with nutrition, Robin helps you with the gym, and your goal is you want to be quicker. Four weeks later, we put you on a scale again, and I blindfold you. And If I ask her how she's feeling, she would say she feels the best I've ever felt. And then we looked at your speed scores and she has improved, she has hit PBs [personal bests] in the gym, and you're the quickest you've ever been. But then I'll tell you, you're three kilos heavier. Are you bothered or not?"'

As well as weight, James can use body composition testing to see how much of a player's weight is muscle, fat, bones or organs. 'When I do the body comps, I try to put myself in the girls' shoes,' James says. 'There's a man coming into camp, and he wants to skinfold, and that can be quite scary. So I don't push it on to anyone. Once you've built that trust up with the players, they actually come forward and want to engage with those metrics. I talk all the time about how we will get the players to be the most functional players they can possibly be and use that to assess them, rather than the number on the metrics.'

James worked with the England women's football team for 18 months and found similar issues with some players being concerned about their weight. The difference in football is that the players were mostly very slim, so the challenge for James there was making them stronger. 'The more muscular legs you have, the higher you're going to jump and the quicker you're going to be. But for some of those girls, they've played at 55kg to 60kg their whole lives and they didn't want to go to 62kg. So that's where my reframing of weight and body mass becomes functional. That was a big project with the Lionesses.

'Now, if you look at Lucy Bronze [a Lioness], she's one of the strongest players. She's got one of the best body comps and she's one of the quickest players. If you asked her what she weighs, she would say, "I don't know, I don't care." Now for me that is an amazing role model moment. She's currently the best player in the world – the strongest, the quickest, the fastest. She is the one that buys into nutrition the most. She eats really well and she's not bothered about what her weight is.'

There are three plans that players are on. Maximisers are expected to put on weight, minimisers are encouraged to lose weight, and maintainers should stay the same. A player can expect to be on different plans at different times depending on their goal. 'There might be some people that have been put in certain groups if they think there is a performance element to their weight,' Sarah Bern explains. 'They might say they want you to be a bit more dynamic so they will put you in the minimisers until you hit this weight, or they might want you to be more of a ball-carrying threat, so they're going to put you in the maximisers until you gain maybe 2kg. It fluctuates.'

How closely do the players follow the meal plans, given they have free range at the buffet? 'It's very much down to the person,' Sarah Bern explains. 'There'll be a few people that don't even look it up. But for me, if I sat down in a meeting, and they ask, "Why haven't you lost weight? Or why have you gained this weight?" I never want to give them the excuse that I didn't follow the meal plan. They might say they have a player happy to follow the nutrition because that's going to be best for the team. So they are going to pick this player.'

According to James, these conversations would not happen; no player would have their weight criticised to such an extent, but it's interesting that the fear is in Sarah's mind. There are a couple of instances in rugby where weight becomes important in the game, and that's for the scrum, the weight of which is important for the coaches, and the jumper in the lineout. 'Naturally with a pack of forwards, the coaches will definitely be keeping an eye on weight because they're looking at the scrum. There are conversations about what weight a player is, but never once in this environment has it been said to the coach that a player needs to put on or lose weight. Never.'

To make sure the players are eating enough, they will be monitored to make sure they are having regular menstrual cycles. 'What I wouldn't want is one of my players to purposely under-fuel. If you've got someone who's chronically under-fuelled, their ability to grow muscle stops or it's reduced, their ability to focus is reduced, their coordination is reduced. Their risk of injury goes up, their ability to have a normal cycle disappears. And one of the key triggers, or one of the key signs of a female athlete that is potentially under-fuelling, is that they haven't had a period for four months, or six months. And alarmingly, in sport, some of these girls think that's normal. And it's kind of down to me and the other staff to detect that. We make it clear to the girls that we would encourage them to have regular healthy cycles.'

A challenge right now is that so little of sports science research is based on women, in part because research on men is relatively easier to control because men do not have a menstrual cycle. The Well HQ, a company that runs courses and consultancy in women's health and science, estimates that only 6 per cent of sports science research is conducted exclusively on women.

As the research develops, there have been changes to how some areas of sport treat women. For example, there is growing evidence that women are more likely to tear ligaments towards the middle of the cycle, near ovulation, because the ligaments have more laxity and are therefore at a higher risk for injury.

The research on nutritional needs at different points of the cycle is in its early stages, so the Red Roses do not change their diets based on where they are in the cycle, but they are advised about what foods or supplements can help them alleviate the symptoms. If a player is a heavy bleeder, the team doctor might test her iron levels and if low, the player can be offered an iron tablet. Players are also offered anti-inflammatory foods that can help players with bloating or inflammation in their body.

Once the trust has been built between James and the players, he is able to build on their performance nutrition in a healthy way that limits the risk of a player eating in a disordered manner. Perhaps the best example of how comfortable the players are with food is that they are happy to eat cakes from a local coffee shop in the same room as James, safe in the knowledge that their relationships with food are about balance, and there is a mutual respect between players and James. But on the whole, the players in England camp are there because they want to be the best players in the world, and performance nutrition is not new to them. At their club they will at least have been educated about the macronutrients in food and how much of each they should be aiming for. Many players say that one of the best parts about coming into England camp is having the nutrition plan sorted for them, and learning more about how it helps them perform.

'With nutrition, you've got 20 to 30 eating opportunities a week, and that's breakfast, lunch, dinner and snacks. And in every one of those eating opportunities, I have the ability to support or negate what the player is trying to achieve. So with Sarah Bern, as an example, if she is trying to put on lean muscle mass and I'm feeding her crap food, she's going to really struggle to do that. If there's another player that wants to drop a little bit of fat mass, because they want to become quicker, and I'm giving them crap carbohydrates and deep-fried foods, they're going to really struggle to do that. And that's where I can directly impact performance. We often say that the best speed coaches are nutritionists because if I can make a player two kilos lighter, then it's a lot easier for them to get to top speed because they're carrying less mass.'

The 72 hours around a game, 36 before and 36 after, are the most important in terms of nutrition. Before a match, James is focused on fuelling the players in the best way possible, which includes a lot of carbohydrates, but also making sure they are mentally in the best place ahead of the match.

'It's so important that we get the preparation right from a fuelling point of view but also a psychological point of view. If they feel good, they're happy,' James says.

'The key macronutrients for a rugby player going into a game are carbohydrates. We're trying to saturate as much glycogen within the muscle as possible, because glycogen is what supports team sport games like rugby, in terms of fuelling. So with that in mind, we're really trying to increase carbohydrate the day before and the day of the game. So Berner [Sarah Bern] really likes to eat pasta the night before, because it's a big carbohydrate meal. She's fuelling her tank up ready. Now, in terms of the target amount, we talked about six grams of carbohydrates per kilo of weight. So if you're a 100kg athlete, you're looking at about 600 grams of carbohydrates. To give you an example of the food equivalent, that'd be 12 jacket potatoes' worth of carbohydrates.

'Let's say they're playing at 3 p.m. on a Saturday. Normally, you would start your carb load on Friday morning, and then you're actively encouraging them to carb up at breakfast. So now we put out pancakes or waffles the day before because the girls enjoy them and they will eat them. Then at lunchtime and snacks, we're encouraging carbohydrates. Dinner is a big carbohydrate dinner because this is normally the last big meal that they're having. So it might be spaghetti bolognese with garlic bread, or something with rice, sweet potatoes or normal potatoes. And then we normally put a dessert on the night before a game. And actively scheduling desserts in the week goes a long way in helping the players mentally. Last week, we had an apple and rhubarb crumble with ice cream. The girls said it was amazing and they were happy customers that night. So as a nutritionist, I'm actively encouraging them to eat those carbs. I want them to go to bed feeling heavy and feeling full because then the magic happens – you let all of the carbohydrates saturate into the muscles, and then they wake up on the day of the game ready to go.'

On the day of the game, players tend to have a light but carb-heavy breakfast. Some players are so nervous on game days that they struggle to eat at all, in which case James will encourage them to sip on a carb-loaded smoothie. On match days, players are offered cereals, oats, bananas, toasts, jams, honey or waffles, all carb-heavy foods which help fuel their muscles. That last pre-match meal tends to be around three and a half hours before kick-off to allow the food to digest.

In the changing room, James and the team will have all the supplements ready including energy and caffeine gels.

'Sometimes players will arrive to the changing room and they might have half a banana, they might snack on a few sweets or they might want a Jaffa Cake. So there are some options there if players want to have a little nibble. We then have an array of supplements ranging from creatine, which helps build muscle mass, to beta alanine, which acts as a little bit of a buffer to lactic acid build-up.'

If you have ever watched the Red Roses sing the national anthem and wondered why they are all chewing gum, it's because they are getting one final boost of caffeine before the game begins. Caffeine is an important part of preparing players for the match. 'We have carbohydrate gels, caffeine gels, caffeine gum. If it's a liquid form of caffeine, like an energy drink or a gel, we would advise the girls that if they want one before the game, to have that about 30 to 45 minutes before the game, because it takes a little bit of time for that to be digested and get into the circulation. If they're having a caffeinated gum, that's far quicker, which is why they have it right before kick-off.'

After the match, James's attention turns to helping the players recover as quickly as possible. In most tournaments there is a tight turnaround between games, so James does all he can to help the players get enough protein and supplements to help their muscles recover. The shakes will have a combination of carbohydrates to replenish their energy stores, protein and creatine which both help muscle repair. The players have protein shakes almost every day and will also have night-time protein called casein, which is a slow-release variant which helps the body recover during sleep.

The players also take health and immunity supplements including vitamin D, zinc, vitamin C and iron tablets for those that need them. It's a packed nutrition schedule and it can be a struggle for players. Jess Breach says that drinking protein shakes before bed is not always enjoyable, and for many players being in camp means consuming more food and shakes than they are used to at home.

Not only is it a change in the volume of food they consume, but also the food is different and players can find it difficult to eat whatever food has been organised for them. James wants the food to be appealing so that the players will eat enough of it, but pleasing all of them can be tricky.

Sarah Bern explains that the team have been having rice pudding lately and some bao buns. 'They're banging, actually,' says Delaney Burns, the England forward. The players have favourite meals in camp and look forward to the week's menu being announced.

'You pick up on things that they like and don't like,' James says. 'They like chicken thighs, but they don't like it on the bone, so we get boneless thighs now. It's just understanding what they enjoy, so a good example with the Roses now is that whatever meat or fish we put on, it might have a black bean sauce, for example; we will always cook three plain portions of that meat in the kitchen ready for players if they ask for it.

'There are little nuances that you pick up with the players like that. Quite often when I email hotels, I will say here's the menu, and then here's some bullet points that if you nail this, you'll have really good feedback from the girls. And a lot of that is the presentation of the food. So I say to the hotels, when you're putting food on, be passionate about how it looks. We eat with our eyes. If it looks great, you're more likely to go on with it.'

That doesn't always go to plan, so when James is in camp he tries to be present at all mealtimes to make sure that the food is being prepared and presented in the best way. He cross-checks it to make sure nothing is being served that shouldn't be, and is around if players have any questions about the food.

There might be the misconception that the role of the nutritionist is to restrict how much players eat and ban them from the biscuit tin. Considering how prevalent eating disorders are in young women, you might question whether it is appropriate for James to be hovering around at mealtimes. It's something I wanted to witness, and I was pleasantly surprised at how comfortable the players are at mealtimes. They eat good portions and don't seem fazed by having staff around. The players are high-performance athletes and they want to be the best they can be, and they are educated on how healthy eating becomes part of that.

There are certainly players who find the food challenging, especially because hotel food is not always high quality, but players such as Jess Breach and Sadia Kabeya say that having a nutritionist in camp, and support throughout the season at club level, has helped heal their relationship with food, rather than add any pressure on to them. At one point, Jess was skipping meals in an attempt to lose weight, and Sadia would under-fuel herself to such a level that she struggled to play rugby. Food is deeply personal and a sensitive part of life and it would be remiss of me to suggest all players have a perfect relationship with it or eat well all the time. As well as a meal out scheduled every week on a Tuesday, players are allowed to order takeaways on certain days in camp or go out for dinner in small groups. James tries to position food as fuel rather than a reward, but recognises the social impact food can have and doesn't stand in the way of players. Instead he encourages them to keep deep-fried food away from match days and instead choose food which will help them achieve their goals.

Alcohol is not banned in camps, but James has never had a player ask if it's OK to have a drink during a tournament. The players are aware of how competitive the environment is, and if a player was to ask James if they could drink, it would signal to him that perhaps they were not committed to the targets of the team. Players hold each other to high standards and there is a collective pressure to make good decisions. The night after a tournament is a different matter. The players can become feral. They love to have a drink together and the RFU often hire out pubs or bars for the players to celebrate. They often have their own nights out, away from staff, to drink well and enjoy each other's company. As my Irish Nana Chris says whenever anybody is on the booze, good luck to them.

The players' fitness is important to make sure they are able to fulfil the jobs asked of them on the rugby pitch. Strength and conditioning is the team's answer to that. 'S&C', as it is known, might make your mind wander towards a gym, full of weights smashing on the floor and muscular giants stomping around. At least that's how scary it sounds to me. Nowadays S&C is as much 'conditioning' as it is 'strength'.

'The days of strength and conditioning being just in the gym are long gone. Now it's about trying to combine as much of the game as we can within our silos,' says Ethan Kinney, who is the lead women's strength and conditioning coach for England. He and Robin Eager, the head of athletic performance for the team, form the S&C department. Their aim is to help players' bodies prepare for Test-level rugby. Fitness is a large part of what they do, but so are mobility exercises and helping players' ankles prepare to play on 4G pitches.

'The point of S&C in any sport is training individuals to meet the demands of this sport, and try to exceed the demands as well,' Ethan says. 'Because essentially, we don't want players going into games who aren't strong enough, aren't fit enough and aren't conditioned to play the game. So it's about making players robust, healthy, strong and fast enough for the Test-level environment.

'Our big thing is that we want to train high and play low. We want to train above the demands of the game so when we do play it will feel like it's easy. We don't want to see players with their hands on their knees, blowing, in a match. But we'll do that in training, because that's where we want to take them to. We stress different areas of the game in training, which will be above and beyond what they would experience out on the pitch on a game day.'

The players all have access to S&C coaches at the club level, who help the team stay at an athletic level of fitness. Robin and Ethan will monitor their performances at club level and check in with each club's S&C department to make sure each player is on target to be fit enough for the England camps.

The pair have to keep up with all Premiership Women's Rugby clubs who have England players, so Ethan takes all clubs along the west of the country and Robin takes the east side. They can then check in with the staff and the players at the clubs and make sure they are training to a high standard. 'We use GPS to track all their players while they are at their club,' Ethan says. 'So if we see players falling down in terms of on-feet time, we can talk to club physios and try and make sure they are getting all they need. The gap between the clubs and internationals can be quite big at times, so it's about keeping on top of that.'

When the players get into an England camp, Robin and Ethan keep the programme simple and consistent, so as not to overload players with new training. 'Simplicity is often the best form of training; training doesn't need to be overly complicated,' Ethan says. 'These athletes haven't been professional athletes for the last 20 years like the men have. You've always got to respect that they are new female athletes, and they are still developing. A young male player might have been doing S&C since he was 16 years old, whereas for women it's probably just started in the last two or three years.'

There's a mix of gym work and on-pitch training for the players. The team have three gym sessions a week, which was lowered to two in the Rugby World Cup due to the tight turnarounds between games. 'We don't want gym athletes, we want athletic rugby players,' Ethan says, 'not someone who can only lift weights. We want them to be able to run, express balls fast, pass off both hands and be robust.'

The team will have an upper body training session on Monday. The lower body is rested on Monday, a part of the routine introduced when the players have had a game at the weekend. In this session, players focus on building strength and move slowly between the exercises, which they track via an app on their phones. The atmosphere in the gym on Monday tends to be buoyant as the players have come back from a rest day on the Sunday. The spirits are high and the music is pumping. Through the speakers blasts music normally confined to a Popworld dance floor. Marlie Packer cannot resist singing along to 'Flowers' by Miley Cyrus, and Hannah Botterman can stop the whole gym with a dance. It's the most relaxed gym session of the week.

Tuesday is the hardest session. With all components of England's training schedules, they like to block the hard work together so that days off can be properly enjoyed. Ethan says that this method helps the players understand when to switch on and switch off and also expose players to physical and mental fatigue. In that lower body session, the team are expected to lift heavy weights and work hard to reach personal bests. The session is gruelling.

On the pitch, Tuesday's session is focused on acceleration, changing direction and collisions. Ethan might shorten the length of the pitch and narrow its sides and make the team play in a smaller area, leading to more collisions, to prepare for a match of repetitive collisions – such as France. This drill tests how quickly players can recover from a tackle and go again. The ball is quickly recycled and hardly moves. Then Ethan might go back to a full-size pitch and test the players' speed once given the space to run around each other. 'We want to be, as much as we can, a rugby environment,' Ethan says. 'Because we respect the rugby conditioning and that means trying to condition players within a rugby environment.'

Thursday's session is short and sharp, around 20 minutes long, and the focus is on speed and power. The team does exercises like power cleans and box jumps to sharpen up their agility and strength.

As the week progresses, it's interesting to see how people's body language changes too. On Monday, the team are chatty in the gym and laughing with each other. On Thursday, the team are quiet, some with headphones in, most not talking to each other. There's a focus to Thursday's session; everything needs to be fast and powerful. There will be time to catch up later.

Wednesdays are for 'growing the gap' between England and their competitors, and in terms of S&C that can mean improving the players' mobility, which helps with all areas of their game. 'We're trying to teach the players 20–25 mobility exercises that they can do themselves at any time, and that could end up being the 1 per cent difference that makes them better,' Ethan says.

The concept of the 1 per cent improvements is a theme throughout the camp. The staff talk about the '1 per cent difference' that will help the team lift the 2025 Rugby World Cup. The S&C team's role in that mission is to make players' bodies fit and strong enough to withstand the pressure of the Test-level environment, so they perform well and are not injured.

'We play on lots of different surfaces, so for example playing on a 4G pitch [synthetic turf] is different to playing on grass, and we don't want that difference to be the thing that breaks us,' Ethan says. 'Training on a 4G, with the rubber crumb, is more stressful on your Achilles than a grass pitch, because grass has more give. So if we're playing on a 4G pitch, the team will dial back jumps and skips in the gym because we know they are going to get exposed to that potential stress more.'

Emily Ross, the lead physiotherapist for the Red Roses,

England line up to sing the national anthem before the 2010 Rugby World Cup final against New Zealand. Simon Balson/Alamy Stock Photo

The England team celebrate winning the 2014 Rugby World Cup. In the centre of the bottom row, Katy Daley-McLean lifts the trophy 20 years after England last won it. On the far left, in the bottom row, is head coach Gary Street. Action Plus Sports/Alamy Live News

Heartbreak as the World Cup is no longer England's. Captain Sarah Hunter hugs Abbie Ward (then known as Abbie Scott) as New Zealand celebrate winning the 2017 Rugby World Cup. Brian Lawless/PA images

A similar tale, five years later. Marlie Packer and Emily Scarratt console each other moments after the final whistle has blown in the 2021 Rugby World Cup (played in 2022) final. New Zealand beat England 34–31. Centre right is Ellie Kildunne, the Red Rose and photographer who shot some of the photos in these pages. Andrew Cornaga/Photosport via AP

Sarah Bern runs with the ball against Australia in the quarter-final of the 2021 Rugby World Cup. Here you can see just how wet the conditions were and how soaked their kit is.
Brett Phibbs/PA Images

The team go to waterfalls in New Zealand on a day off during the 2021 Rugby World Cup. From left to right, top row: Ellie Kildunne, Helena Rowland, Lydia Thompson, Alex Matthews, Maud Muir, Morwenna Talling. Bottom row: Rosie Galligan, Claudia MacDonald, Vickii Cornborough, Abby Dow. Ellie Kildunne, Red Rose and photographer

Maud Muir looks surprised as she scores a try in the 2023 Women's Six Nations match against Wales at the Cardiff Arms Park. The Red Roses won 59–3. Andrew Orchard/ Alamy Live News

Alex Matthews scores for England as they beat France in the 2023 Women's Six Nations in front of 58,498 fans, a record crowd for a women's rugby fixture. England won 38–33. Mark Pain/Alamy Live News

Sarah Bern smiles from the sidelines as she watches the team practise their lineouts.
Ellie Kildunne, Red Rose and photographer

Life in a Red Roses camp. Mo Hunt, left, makes Marlie Packer laugh as the team gets changed for a training session. Ellie Kildunne, Red Rose and photographer

Mo Hunt and Helena Rowland do some training work in the gym during a power session with the backs. Music is blaring and the team are working on explosive movements.
Ellie Kildunne, Red Rose and photographer

A pretty good six-a-side football team meet in England's 2023 Six Nations camp. Many of the players used to play football as children and enjoy the chance to have a kickabout during camp. From left to right, back row: Abbie Ward (around five-months pregnant here), Marlie Packer and Sarah Hunter. Front row: Poppy Cleall, Mo Hunt and Rosie Galligan.
Ellie Kildunne, Red Rose and photographer

Jess Breach in a laughing fit during a game of fives in the England camp as the team are in New Zealand for the 2023 WXV1 tournament. There are lots of close friendships within the team and plenty of silly moments. Ellie Kildunne, Red Rose and photographer

A new era begins. Marlie Packer leads her team out in the inaugural WXV1 competition, in the autumn of 2023. The Red Roses won the tournament, beating New Zealand 33–12 in the final match. Joe Serci/SPP

Louis Deacon (left) and John Mitchell (right) discuss the England team after they play Australia at the WXV1 competition. Louis was working as the interim coach before John took over. Ellie Kildunne, Red Rose and photographer

Jubilant scenes in the changing room as England celebrate their WXV1 victory. Beer is flying in the air and the team are singing and dancing: two things they love to do.
Ellie Kildunne, Red Rose and photographer

leads the mobility sessions with the players, who are chatting away while stretching on the floor of the team's hotel. It's moments like that which remind her why she has always wanted to work in rugby. 'It's probably the bits in between my job that I enjoy the most,' she says. 'The camaraderie, the silliness – those are the amazing bits.'

Her love for rugby came before a desire to be a physiotherapist. When Emily was a young child, her dad would take her and her sister to watch London Irish play and the two children would sit on the advertising boards and share a portion of chips. She got to see players up close and felt inspired by London Irish players Conor O'Shea (who is now the executive director of performance for England Rugby, and therefore her head of department), and Justin Bishop. Emily's parents thought she might become a teacher or a nurse and she likes to think her job is in the middle of the two, as she gets to teach players about their bodies every day.

'They say if you love your job, you never work a day in your life,' she says. 'There are definitely moments of high stress and high focus, but there are lots of silly moments which are wonderful. Like the chats you have in the medical room, or in the gym, all of those bits make the job enjoyable. Those connections you make with players are great because you're helping them learn more about their bodies.'

As Emily gained experience in physiotherapy from a range of different sports, she was intrigued by the opportunity to work in the high-performance environment of the Red Roses. 'I wanted to work at a level of excellence, with a level of innovation and challenge that wasn't just me firefighting,' she says. 'I want to make a difference as a physio or want to be able to affect change.'

England's re-injury rate is very low, and the team's training availability is high, which are two good signs that Emily's work is good. 'Usually when we rehabilitate somebody with an injury, they never come back with the same injury, which is really significant,' she says. The most common injury is concussion, followed by knee and ankle injuries.

The best example of Emily's physiotherapy ingenuity is the miraculous return of Abby Dow, who with Emily's guidance recovered from a horrific leg break during the 2022 Women's Six Nations. Abby was playing against Wales when a tackle caused her to break her right leg at the top and bottom, only six months away from that year's World Cup. She was told that it was extremely unlikely she would make the World Cup as she needed major surgery on her leg. Recovery from such a break usually takes nine months, but Emily – whom Abby describes as a 'witch doctor' – created an intense rehab plan for Abby and managed to get her fit for the World Cup in only six months.

Emily and her small team of physiotherapists can also proactively make players more robust to minimise the risk of injury and help them recover faster. 'You can change the systems that help but you can't actually stop an injury,' she says. 'So whenever we have injuries, we will always look back and see if it was modifiable and if there was anything we could have done to stop it. If it's a non-modifiable injury, like a contact injury, we accept that it is rugby and those injuries are going to happen. But we can also prepare players better for contact sessions so they're ready for it, and we can expose them to enough contact so they're more durable and the contact injuries should go down.'

Her role is not a nine-to-five job and a good day in an

England camp could begin at 7.30 a.m. and finish at 9.30 p.m., demanding excellent commitment to the cause. 'I'm always just trying to find ways to keep great players doing what they are doing,' Emily says. 'If I can improve in any way, shape or form by 1 per cent, then I'll try and improve it. They're great players anyway, but if you can make them fitter, faster or stronger overall, you'll win, and they'll become less injured. Physically, they're able to sustain a bigger tackle, they're able to fall better, they're able to get that bit further without a leg strain; it all adds up in the end.'

In camps it's important to get them into a routine as quickly as possible. 'They come from clubs that all do things in a different way,' she says. 'To build consistency and intensity through the weeks, we have to be quite heavy on the routine, which for me is injury prevention in itself. So probably one of the biggest challenges is matting together the routines from all the different clubs and the slight nuances of how they do stuff.'

Once the players are settled into the routine, Emily focuses as much on teaching the players about their bodies and injuries as she does treating them. 'The thing that you notice when you're in camps versus when they are in clubs is the consistency of communication, decision-making and intensity,' Emily explains. 'We consistently try to mirror their training load to the game demands. They constantly go through that loop and they know it well. They're finely tuned in the sense that you can't just add 30 minutes on to a training session, or just add two sessions in a day.'

The team behind the team are the unsung heroes, helping the players on their quests for the 1 per cent advantages they talk about so often. It's the invisible work that most fans don't see that adds up to equal success. From nutrition to psychology, the staff make sure that the players who line up to sing the national anthem are in the best condition possible, with only their game plan to focus on. What happens next, after the anthem is sung and the whistle is blown, is the responsibility of the coaching team. So how do you reach a 30-match unbeaten streak?

Chapter 5

MORE THAN A MAUL

England have a unique advantage. Their domestic competition, the Premiership Women's Rugby (previously known as the Premier 15s), is the most competitive women's rugby league in the world and gives England players exposure to high level rugby week in, week out. The vast majority of the players' training comes from the clubs, who are increasingly linked with men's Premiership clubs and therefore have access to great facilities and top-level coaching. The high-performance environments at clubs offer daily monitoring and training for players and some clubs offer additional support such as nutrition advice. The result is a competitive market for the England coaches to go shopping for players. But when those players make the step up to the international stage, it can be a completely different kettle of fish, despite it being, technically speaking, a higher level of high performance.

Creating a high-performance environment in the England women's rugby team is difficult by the very nature of the camps. They are hugely intense and competitive environments which can be painful at times, and fostering a good atmosphere requires a delicate balance of challenge and

119

support. Players must raise their game and never settle, outside of the comfort they might feel at their clubs. It also takes time for all the elements of high performance to come together in the short, sharp blocks of training camps.

For Scott Bemand, the team's attack coach from 2015 to 2023 who later became the head coach of Ireland Women, the comfort zone is the enemy of high performance. To excel in the increasingly competitive world of rugby, the team must constantly push beyond their current capabilities and not rest on their laurels. 'If it's just nice, that's not high performance because that sits below the line of actually getting better,' he says. 'If you're just good or better than other people, how do you get even better if you sit below that line? You just sit there and it's nice, it's comfortable, people are probably happy. But when everybody else in the room is trying to get better, you have to keep striving for better every day. So there's an awful lot of work going into that.'

To achieve this in a way that doesn't lead to burnout, the players must also feel completely supported – not comfortable – in the camps. It's a tricky balance for the coaches to get right. Coaches should not be the most popular figures in the camp, Scott believes. They are the ones who have to have the difficult conversations about selection decisions or poor performances, a task the coaches always find a challenge. Even players who are regarded as the best in the world in their positions have to be faced with uncomfortable truths and have to be pushed outside their comfort zones. It's the only way to get better.

However, alongside those challenging conversations, a deep level of support is essential. The coaching staff must offer unwavering support to the players, both as individuals and within the broader support network. This support is crucial in creating an environment where players feel secure to take risks, make mistakes and learn from them. It is through this combination of challenge and support that players can reach their highest potential, according to Scott.

Trust is the crux that holds such a precariously balanced environment together. Scott refers to it as the 'pinnacle' of the relationship between the coaching staff and the players. Trust allows for open communication and mutual respect. Players must trust that the coaching staff's challenges and feedback are rooted in their best interests and aimed at the shared goal of success, and staff must trust players to listen to their guidance.

Creating mutual ground between the players and the coaches has sometimes been an issue. The head coach of England has always been a man, and as is the case of new coach John Mitchell and former head coach Simon Middleton, they are men with a solid background in the men's game.

Interestingly, every coach and coach educator I spoke to raised the same points when explaining the difference between coaching women compared to coaching men. It sounds like a generalisation, borderline sexist at points, but that's not how it should be read. The number one difference, according to every single coach, is the need to explain the *why*. Why are we doing tackle practice today? Why is there one more player on that team? Why can't we do some lineout work instead?

'The "why" is really important to them,' Simon says. 'You can't just tell them to do something and they'll just do it. They need to know why they are doing it too. Which is good because they want to understand, but it can get in the way a bit too. That is definitely one of them [a way that coaching women is different to coaching men], without a doubt,' he says, in the tone of someone who has been exasperated by questions during training sessions.

'Don't get me wrong, some of the best performances we have had are from when we've told the players to listen, and just do as we say. They'll do it and they'll do it brilliantly. And I think sometimes they like just being told what to do, they need that clarity, and to know it's not the time for questions. But yes, that understanding, the "why?" questions, are a huge part of the game.'

The backchat from players led to the coaches adopting training scenarios where only one player in each group can talk to the coaches. This was partly to replicate what happens on the pitch where only the captain should approach the referee, and partly to give the coaches a break from answering questions. During a World Cup warm-up training session, the team trained with those rules and there was a sin bin on the side of the training pitch. Forwards coach Louis Deacon sent an entire team to the bin at one point, letting the other team score end-to-end tries while their opposition were in the bin. Any guesses for who the players are that give the most backchat? The team consisted of the scrum halves in the camp (Leanne Infante, Lucy Packer and Mo Hunt). Louis also gives honourable mentions to backchat queens Marlie Packer and Poppy Cleall.

'The biggest difference [with the men's game] is the attention to detail and they want to know why,' Louis says. 'I can tell them we're doing something but they'll really want to dig into the why and they ask a lot more questions [than male rugby players]. I remember in that first training session, Midds [Simon Middleton] warned me that they would have loads of questions, so I told the girls that we were there to work, we're going to train really fast and intensely, and then we can ask questions once we're finished. It sort of changed the approach, whereas if I had gone into that session and asked if there were any questions, there would be loads of hands going up. But I really think it's a good thing because it's the attention to detail. They want to do things really well, and want to know why they're doing things.'

The reason behind the 'why' is important to understand. For years, the women had to advocate for themselves and often took ownership of their training plans. At clubs, as some of the best and most experienced players, they have had a say in how things are done and like to feel included in the set-up.

Simon is quite honest that working with so many women was a learning curve for him, and not a job he has always got right. One of the biggest lessons was understanding how he could help build the confidence of his players.

Kate Hayes, the team's former psychologist who had vast experience in the men's and women's game, gave Simon valuable insight into how the women differed from men in terms of the feedback and praise they needed. 'She said that men don't really need their coach to tell them that they had a great game or they played fantastic out there. They know, and they will feed off their own reflections and their own thoughts about their own performance. But the girls could be outstanding, but unless you say, "You played outstanding today," or, "That was a great piece of play," they won't believe it. They need to hear it from coaches because they feed off the coaches' support and that helps build their confidence back.

'It was a real penny drop moment for me; a real eye-opener. And as soon as Kate said it, I thought, "Yes, that is absolutely true."'

The differences between men's and women's coaching doesn't stop there. Gary Street, the 2014 Rugby World Cup-winning coach, remembers when a misunderstanding between the players and Stuart Pickering, the strength and conditioning coach, threatened the team's preparation for the 2014 Rugby World Cup. Gary asked Stuart to work with the team after he heard he was the most savage fitness coach in rugby. Stuart had not worked with women's rugby players before but he keenly took up the role. He implemented a rule that players could not appear tired during training sessions, as such body language gives power to the opposition in matches, so the players were not allowed to put their hands on their heads or on their knees. No matter what point of their training session the team were in, if they were caught looking tired, they had to start the whole session again.

Two and a half hours into one brutal fitness session, Stuart blew his whistle and made the players start the session again, saying he had seen multiple players with their hands on their heads. The players protested that nobody had done that, but such arguments were futile. They were sent back to the start of the session, and by the end of the day, the players were exhausted and furious. A couple of them approached Gary to tell him that it was unfair. They believed Stuart had lied about seeing players with their hands on their heads, that he had done it just to punish them, and that such behaviour went against their culture of trust. Gary was alarmed and spoke to Stuart about how important fairness and honesty was to women's rugby players, and encouraged him to apologise to the players. Stuart said he was certain they had put their hands on their heads. He was not budging from his view as he knew what he had seen. So Gary had no choice but to review the video footage of the session, aware that he had a mutiny on his hands. He found that neither side was lying. The players weren't putting their hands on their heads, they were sorting out their hair scrunchies.

There are many shocking factors for men who join women's rugby clubs for the first time. From learning to knock before going into the changing room for a half-time talk to understanding the menstrual cycle, it can certainly be a sharp learning curve. There is also huge potential, especially with the Red Roses, and coaches often remark about being surprised by the quality of the rugby. 'I remember my first session,' Louis says. 'As a new coach coming in you don't want to do what has been done in the past, you want to do your own thing. I was blown away by how quickly they all picked it up. Literally in one session. Their attention to detail and all those sorts of things are what sets them apart. I was very impressed and surprised.'

The players know their own positions and strengths well and a group of the team's leaders work cohesively with the coaches to create the game plans. The strategy group, as they are known, includes the captain, vice-captain and key decision-makers in the team such as the scrum leader, lineout leader, scrum half and a defensive leader. These players will regularly meet with the coaching team to discuss the on-field tactics that the team adopt in each game.

The collaboration between players and coaches within the strategy group has become integral to the team's success.

The team use their analyst, Calum Gilbert, to help inform those meetings. As the sole analyst dedicated to the team, his responsibilities involve helping the Red Roses prepare for matches, including helping strategy group players analyse areas of interest, and helping individual players fine-tune aspects of their game.

Calum works closely with each coach and tailors his analysis to their specific requirements. The head coach relies on Calum for comprehensive team perspective analysis, such as the data from England's previous matches and what the statistics say about their next opponent, as well as the data about individual players. Calum would then collaborate closely with Louis Deacon, focusing on the intricacies of the set piece and the forwards, and with the backs coach, honing in on the backs' performance, particularly emphasising first-phase strikes and first-phase defence.

With an abundance of data at his disposal, Calum's challenge lies in effectively filtering and presenting information to the players and coaching staff. Aware that overwhelming players with excessive data can hinder their decision-making on the field, Calum's goal is to provide specific, actionable insights to players that can be used to assist decisions on the field.

But perhaps the most interesting part of Calum's role is how he supports the coaches to make real-time decisions during matches. He provides them with the necessary information as the match is ongoing, enabling them to make big calls both in the heat of the moment and during half-time conversations in the changing room.

One of Calum's primary responsibilities during matches is to track key statistics such as possession, territory, penalties and turnovers. By monitoring these metrics closely, he can identify trends and patterns that are often hidden within the fervour of rugby, which provide valuable insights into the team's performance. For instance, during a match against Wales in the 2023 Women's Six Nations, Louis turned to Calum near the end of the first half and asked about the number of turnovers the team had lost. Calum told him that the team had already lost five turnovers at the breakdown. This information was significant, as in previous games the team had not relinquished any turnovers in that area. It gave the coaches the data to be able to present to the players at half-time in order to improve their performance at the breakdown in the second half. In short, Calum's data analysis allows the coaches to highlight specific issues and devise strategies to rectify them in real time.

Calum recognises that not all players have the same approach to data and analysis. Some players prefer a more simplified approach, where Calum can serve as a sounding board for their ideas, and someone to air their concerns to. For those players, he will try not to overwhelm them with a lot of data.

On the other hand, some players thrive on the intricacies of data analysis, and this is particularly the case with strategy group members. They crave detailed information and find value in exploring the nuances of the game. Calum mentions Abbie Ward as an example of a player who likes to dig into the stats of the set piece and work out small ways she can improve her game. For players like Abbie, and Marlie Packer is another name on that team sheet, Calum tailors his approach to ensure they receive as much detail as they need.

'Cal is great,' Abbie says. 'He'll put together packages of footage that I can look at, on my own laptop, as well as a lot of stats. But I think it's important that you've got to put the actual footage with the stats, because the stats might tell you one thing, but then if you've got eyes on, you can see something else.

'I'll be looking at the opposition's lineout in attack and defence, the personnel and their traits too. A lot of it is characteristics that you can pick up that will be little tells, or how you might manipulate certain people. So that works in both attack and defence around the lineout and around the maul, but also then how that can influence bigger picture things in terms of team plays or where you might want to exploit a team.'

In the build-up to a match, Marlie's role in the strategy group is particularly focused on the breakdown and the set piece, so Calum will create a package of videos that show how her opponents operate at the set piece, or how they tend to lose the ball in the breakdown. Marlie will then go away and forensically study her opposition, and will then raise what she has noticed, with Calum's assistance, in the strategy group meeting before the match. The same will go for many players in the team who refer to Calum for analysis support.

To ensure that the players grasp the concepts and adapt to the opposition's style of play, Calum curates video clips that illustrate how the England team previously confronted the same opposition, or the same challenges they expect to face against that week's opponents. These video clips are made readily available and easily accessible throughout the team environment. Screens displaying the video clips rotate continuously in areas like the team's dining room, allowing players to engage with the material whenever it piques their interest, including during mealtimes. By incorporating video analysis into the players' daily routines, the England team have a constant exposure to the opposition's tactics. This repetitive exposure reinforces the players' familiarity with the opposition's strengths and weaknesses which makes it easier for them to make instinctive decisions on the field.

'Say we've got a game coming up, every one of us in the strategy group will do our own analysis,' Marlie says. 'We'll come into the strat group, talk about the game that we're about to play, and what we've seen in our individual analysis. We'll discuss their attack, defence, set piece, and maybe plays they often do, and then we make our game plan.'

'What's important is everyone has different areas that they kind of take care of,' Abbie adds. 'And then we come together as one group, and we have a full picture. Because you can't do a deep dive into absolutely everything. I look after the lineout, Sarah Bern will look heavily into the scrum, and Marlie might look massively into how they defend, which would inform how we might attack. Someone else might look at how they attack, then, which would inform how we defend. It's nice, because we come together and have a really full picture.'

For the coaches, the strategy group is a chance for them to use the players' expertise in their areas. 'The strategy group was very much about our on-field stuff,' Simon says. 'How we play, tactical decisions, the tactical driving of the side, and that was an area that the players absolutely loved.

The players play rugby for a reason – because they love the game. They want to grow their knowledge of the game and they want to grow their ability. The players who were in that group worked really hard on understanding the game and understanding the opposition, and the results of their actions on the field – if you do this, this will happen, and if we play this way, this is what we would try to get.'

Together, they closely examine on-field practices, protocols and game understanding. The group facilitates open discussions, exchanging ideas on training approaches and evaluating their effectiveness. Players report that being part of the group gives them a sense of ownership for their specialised position and helps them feel more equipped to take on important decisions on the field. The inclusive approach to the overall strategy also fostered a sense of shared responsibility for the results of the team.

'After the game, we'll review the game plan and see if we got it right,' Marlie says. 'And then we can see if we need to change something.' When England played Fiji in the opening game of the 2021 Rugby World Cup, the strategy group identified in their review that England were not presenting the ball fast enough after a ruck. 'Our ball presentation wasn't fast enough and that's an easy fix. So we put into our game plan a buzzword, 'snapback', and we can say it on the pitch,' Marlie explains. 'That got sent out to the girls, and those in the strat group made sure to use it in training before the next match. If we're using the right terminology in training, that carries across to the game.'

For the coaches, the strategy group is a useful way of making sure the players are confident enough to make those decisions under pressure on the field. 'As coaches you want to develop the players' decision-making and responsibility because ultimately, when they get on the field they are the ones who are going to make those decisions,' Simon explains. 'Coaches can have a bit of influence but if you can influence the decisions that are made in the moments that matter on the field, then you've got something good working. And the strategy group had a huge part in preparing to play against opposition, reviewing how we train, chatting about how we might want to train and what worked, what didn't work. You want to give ownership to players. In the whole modern society, it's not about being told what to do any more. It's about sharing information and understanding that if you want responsibility for something, then you have to be prepared to take the accountability that goes with it.'

As Simon stepped away from England, he reflected that the strategy group had helped players prepare for a transition to coaching upon retirement, should they want to. He used the strategy group to expose players to coaching decisions and increase their tactical understanding of the game, with an eye on developing great coaches.

John Mitchell, England's current head coach, took over the England job with no previous experience of coaching women. But what he brings, as did Simon, Louis and Scott, is a wealth of experience in the men's game which particularly lends itself to how the Red Roses play rugby. Simon describes his role as more of a director of rugby than a head coach. He was in charge of managing staff and players, and having the final say on things, but his role was more on a strategic level rather than handling day-to-day training sessions, which is the role John is expected to continue. His task is clear: go one step further and win the Rugby World

Cup in 2025. To do that, he must first set his mark on England's playing style.

The Red Roses' style of rugby can be characterised by their dominant set piece and a flair for beautiful finishing. In attack, England typically play a structured and organised game that focuses on building phases, retaining possession and patiently working their way up the field. The star of the show is England's pushing game – the scrum and the maul – which have become a key focus of the attack. The man responsible is Louis, who was part of the Leicester Tigers team of the noughties who revolutionised the maul to be a relentless weapon used to tear apart defences. When he joined the England squad as the forwards coach in 2021, he wanted to put a focus on the maul as a lethal weapon. England have long been a team who score from the maul, but Louis's greater focus on it has created an almost unstoppable try-scoring tactic for England. Spoiler alert for the next part: England are *really* good at mauling.

'It's a very English way to play, heavily focused on the set piece, but it also comes down to the type of players we have got,' Louis says. 'There's no point focusing your game around a set piece if you've not got forwards that can deliver. We're very blessed from that point of view; we have very technically strong forwards. I think that's probably why we are where we are, because we have those sorts of quality players.

'We've got the likes of Abbie Ward and Zoe Aldcroft who, from a tactical point of view, are some of the best players – men or women – that I've come across. That's from a game understanding point of view and the skill as well. The women's game hasn't been professional for as long as the men's game so for them to be where they are at this stage is a hugely positive thing.'

The driving maul is the most lethal weapon in the arsenal of the Red Roses. Known in camp as the Tank, this set-piece move has become synonymous with their attacking style. With a blend of precision, power and coordination, England have mastered the art of executing a devastating driving maul, often leaving their opponents scrambling to find an answer.

The Tank is unleashed when England win a lineout near the opposition's try line. The forwards assemble as a unified force, tightly binding together with the ball carrier securely placed at the rear. As the call is made and the ball is delivered, the Tank begins its relentless surge forward. Once the maul is passed the try line, the ball-carrying player puts the ball down to score the try.

The sheer physicality of the players propels the maul forward, inch by inch, towards the try line, but it is not just raw power that defines England's driving maul. It is the intelligence and adaptability of the players within the maul that truly make it such a formidable weapon. As the maul rolls on, England can make subtle adjustments, exploiting gaps or shifting the point of attack.

The result is a wave of momentum that is difficult to withstand. Tries are scored, records are broken and victories are sealed as the Tank rumbles on. The England women's team has honed this weapon to such a degree that it has become a symbol of their dominance and a nightmare for their opponents.

England have often been criticised by the media and fans for being too reliant on the lineout driving maul. The criticism peaked at the 2021 Rugby World Cup (played in 2022), but it really began in the 2022 Six Nations, when 27 of the side's 45 tries were scored by forwards. The Tank is England's super strength, but too much analysis of the maul misses a key element of England's attack – the 'stress and stretch' tactic that often leads up to the lineouts in the first place. By constantly moving the ball around and shifting the point of attack, England aim to create defensive disarray and force their opponents into making mistakes. This dynamic allows England to stress the defence by continually changing the direction of play and stretching their opponents' defensive structures until penalties are conceded, which then lead to penalties and lineouts.

'The "push game" [scrums and mauls] is a fundamental and important part culturally of the English game anyway,' Scott says, agreeing with Louis's earlier point. 'But we had the other side of the game as well; it's just that we had an enormous amount of success with the push side of the game so that got all the spotlight really, and people assumed that we were just trying to play that style of game.

'If anybody watched us train, they would know we were using "stress and stretch". One is complementary to the other, so if I'm going to wear you down, I need to move you around. So I want to go over there, and you have to defend, so now I'm gonna move you back over there, they've got to move again, and soon they feel like they're playing on toffee. I'm going to kick it back, and you're going to move back there.

'So we're looking to move teams around with stress and stretch. But quite often, that led to a penalty, which led to the kick to the corner, which led to a lineout driving maul, which led to a try.'

One player who often scores from the maul is prop Sarah Bern, who is one of the most dynamic props in women's rugby. She finds criticism of England's attack irritating and believes women are expected to entertain on a rugby pitch more than men. She wants to focus on results.

'If it's keeping us winning, I don't see an issue,' she said to me during the 2023 World Cup. 'It might not be the most fun thing to watch. But for me, my role is to scrummage and if I can have an opportunity to make the fun line breaks and score a try, that's brilliant and that's what I love doing, but my actual job is to make sure I can scrum and lineout very well. I want to be the best I can be at that and the best in the world.

'If that's people's views, they're very welcome to have them, but unfortunately I don't think it's going to change anything because we still want to be the best and we're still going to push to be good in our set piece.

'You look at the men's game, it's all functioning around the lineout or the scrum. Just because it's a women's game, I don't believe that it should be any different. It shouldn't be seen as dull or boring, because that's what the men's game comes down to. There are tiny, tiny margins in rugby now. Look at the men's World Cup final [in 2019]. South Africa smashed England in the scrum and that was the game-changing thing.'

England's attack is far from one-dimensional, and any suggestion that the team is wholly reliant on their forwards fails to recognise the world-class talent England possess in the backs. Abby Dow is one of the finest finishers in women's rugby and the speed of Jess Breach, Ellie Kildunne and Claudia MacDonald, to name a few, takes England to greater heights. Then there's the tactical mastery of Mo Hunt, Zoe Harrison, Helena Rowland and Emily Scarratt as well as the sheer power of Tatyana Heard. The team is laced with talent in every position.

To get the most out of that talent, Scott adopted an approach that centres on maximising players' super strengths. His philosophy is that each player possesses a 'dial' that allows them to adjust their focus and attention based on the specific hallmarks of their game. For example, if a player is exceptionally fast, they may rely less on catch-and-pass skills and instead utilise their speed to become a running threat. However, as they face tougher opposition, they need to expand their toolkit by developing other skills such as kicking or passing to maintain their effectiveness. Emily, for example, is a 'triple threat', because she can pass, run and kick to a world-class standard, making her a more difficult opponent on the pitch. Her versatility allows her to adapt her game depending on the situation and makes her harder to defend. There are other players who have one super strength, and the game plan will be built around them. Scott uses Jess to illustrate that point. Coming from an athletics background, the 'Jess Express' brings exceptional speed to the team, so the coaching staff worked on creating space for her on the pitch, allowing her to exploit gaps and run around defenders.

Of course, a player at the highest level of the game cannot rely on only one weapon. As the game develops and women's rugby becomes more competitive, players like Jess can be caught in situations where defending teams target her and restrict her space, aware that such a move significantly limits her game. Jess has put in effort to develop her passing, particularly offloading the ball, and kicking, to complement her blistering pace, which has opened up her skill set to be able to play at full back.

That's partly because Jess has a keen eye for space on a rugby pitch, something which the coaches have trained into the team. The players are taught the importance of playing the space in front of them, rather than defenders, to encourage players to look for space and play confidently rather than focusing on the opposition. Coaches place a premium on off-the-ball movement, emboldening players to actively search for space and support each other in attack, so training drills are often focused on helping players make intelligent plays, either as part of a rehearsed move or as an additional option in attack.

That means the role of the backs in the England women's team is a dynamic and adaptable one, where flexibility and responsiveness to opportunities are key. According to Scott, it's like jazz. In that genre of music, one musician starts the beat and others follow, providing a sound that *some people* even enjoy. There are general principles to follow for the musician, and they must be excellent at their craft, but they must also have the skill to adapt and improvise their music. According to Scott, the principles in how the backs attack are similar.

Unlike the forwards who often engage in more structured and choreographed drills like the lineout, the backs operate in wider spaces and have more freedom to make spontaneous decisions. While they do have a framework of plays they practise on the training field and can pull out of the bag when needed, the nature of their position necessitates the ability to adjust and change their approach on the fly.

This adaptability is essential, as even the most intricately planned backs move may need to be abandoned or modified based on the actions of the opposition.

The concept of 'taking space' plays a pivotal role in the backs' approach. They are constantly scanning the field, analysing the defensive line and identifying gaps or weaknesses to exploit. Scott emphasised the importance of players being proactive and seizing opportunities as they arise. For example, if Zoe Harrison receives the ball and has the plan to get the ball to Tatyana Heard at inside centre, but the defence has anticipated that move and left Zoe undefended, Zoe should play with the confidence to take the space. If Zoe was too focused on playing out of the team's playbook, she could miss the opportunities around her.

The backs' collaboration and cohesion as a unit are crucial to their success, hence the reference to jazz. 'In jazz they harmonise together,' Scott says. 'Somebody starts it and then somebody comes in second, but they're all responding to how other people are playing. So backs have elements where you are essentially responding and adapting to opportunity and threat based on what the player before you did.'

The coaching philosophy for the backs revolves around those principles of improvisation, which Scott calls 'scan, act, adapt'. Each player scans the field for potential opportunities and threats, acts accordingly based on their assessment, and adapts their play in response to the unfolding situation.

To support a more expansive style of play, the coaches and support staff have focused on developing the players' rugby intelligence, enabling them to make split-second decisions that maximise the attacking potential in matches. Strength and conditioning is a crucial part of this training and the weekly speed session during camps is used to support the aim of players keeping up with the attack and assisting the ball carrier's efforts. Ellie Kildunne is an excellent example of someone who tracks the ball and supports the ball carrier, providing them with another option if they need it.

Tactical kicking has also become an increasingly important component of England's play, and the team hope to bring in a specialist kicking coach before the 2025 World Cup. 'We're looking into kicking coaches and a scrum coach from a technical point of view,' Louis says. 'They're big parts of the game now so having those specialist coaches in those areas is really important.

'The game is changing now to where you've got to have more variety in the tactics; you can't just do the same thing all the time, so the ability to coach different skill sets can change the game. There's not a big amount of box kicking in the women's game, but I like that because there's probably too much in the men's game. As the game evolves, and teams get better tactically, the kicking game is really important.'

Well-executed kicks can be used in defence or attack to gain territorial advantage, force the opposition into defensive positions, or set up well-placed attacking opportunities. England have strong kickers on the field who make good decisions in crucial moments, such as choosing when to kick for territory or take shots at goal, but developing this skill across the squad will prove vital in 2025 as other nations catch up with the Red Roses.

Despite the variety in England's style, the Red Roses can resort back to their tried-and-tested Tank when the game situation allows it, and often choose to do so later in matches. It remains an important platform to create opportunities for attack, thanks in part to the world-class operators England can call upon in the forward pack. The result of England's developing style of play is a team who entered the 2021 Rugby World Cup on a streak of 25 wins.

From a perilous driving maul to barnstorming wingers, the evolution of England's attack heading into the World Cup meant they seemed untouchable.

Chapter 6

THE 2021 RUGBY WORLD CUP

'We've got to win it,' Simon said just before the team left to go to New Zealand to play in the 2021 Rugby World Cup. 'This is the best prepared squad with the best strength in depth we've ever had.'

The tournament was postponed by one year because of the coronavirus pandemic. So, in 2022, the Red Roses were five years on from their defeat in the 2017 Rugby World Cup final, had been full-time professional since January 2019 and were on a world record unbeaten streak.

New Zealand, traditionally their closest rivals, had a poor lead-up to the tournament. Partly because of the stricter laws in New Zealand around coronavirus, the Black Ferns had only played 16 Test matches in the same time England had played 45. In the autumn of 2021, New Zealand travelled to England to play the Red Roses twice, and England defeated them by record-breaking margins on successive weekends. The first match, a 43–12 win, set the record for an England win against New Zealand, which they then broke again the following weekend in a 56–15 win. New Zealand also played France twice on the tour, losing 38–13 in the first match and 29–7 in the second. Te Kura

Ngata-Aerengamate, a senior Black Ferns player, posted on social media that she had suffered a mental breakdown following the tour.

A report was launched into the culture of the Black Ferns, which was published in April 2022. It found evidence of favouritism, body-shaming language being used and cultural insensitivities. 'What became clear during the review was that Te Kura's concerns were not isolated and some other players (particularly Māori and Pasifika players) had either experienced similar behaviour by a number of members of management (of 'favouritism', 'ghosting', cultural insensitivities), or had witnessed it, or had been told about it contemporaneously,' the review said.

Whereas England's coaching set-up was established and its leaders experienced, New Zealand faced mass change only six months out from hosting the World Cup. New Zealand Rugby threw money and resources at the team, who turned professional in the February before the tournament. They brought in World Cup-winning All Blacks coaches Wayne Smith, Mike Cron and Sir Graham Henry, and All Blacks legend Dan Carter was helping the team perfect their kicking. But could it be too little too late?

To say the Red Roses were the favourites in the tournament is an understatement. The tournament was predicted, for good reason, to be uncompetitive. Fans on social media questioned the point of it when England would be so dominant throughout.

England went into a series of mini camps on 4 July 2022, giving them three months to prepare before they flew out to New Zealand. These training camps were as much a test of selection and performance as they were to see how players cope away from home and how they recover and prepare for the intense nature of elite training nearly every day for weeks.

At the same time, the players and coaches were being filmed for an ITV documentary called *Wear the Rose: An England Rugby Dream*. The documentary gave viewers insight into the Red Roses' preparation for the World Cup, including the stressful selection process. Of the 37 players in the camp, only 32 would have a seat on the plane.

The more public nature of the build-up to the World Cup resulted in greater scrutiny at team selections, and a more public stage for players to swallow the bitter pill of non-selection. One of those to feel the full wrath of non-selection was scrum half Natasha Hunt, known as Mo.

Mo made her debut for England in 2011 and has become a fan favourite in the Red Roses squad. She is easily recognisable on the pitch for her signature hairstyle: her short blonde hair scraped into a plait up from her neck into a messy high bun atop her head, held together with a brightly coloured scrunchie. By the end of the match there is often more hair out of the bun than in it.

She is well loved by team-mates and is one of the most popular members of the Red Roses squad. Maud Muir, who plays her club rugby alongside Mo at Gloucester-Hartpury, found the older Red Rose a comforting presence in the England camp as someone always happy to have a laugh, often giggling, and available to help players with any issues.

Part of Mo's appeal to fans is her honesty about her own struggles with her mental health. In the build-up to the 2021 Six Nations, Mo had prepared to publicly withdraw from the squad due to her mental health, but an ankle injury forced her out of the squad anyway. She felt like she was dragging energy out of the team, her usually chirpy personality replaced with someone that felt like a shell of herself, unable to hold back the tears and feeling withdrawn from her environment. The downturn in her mental health really came from the coronavirus lockdown. Mo is an extrovert and bounces off other people's energy, so having a mandated two-metre gap away from her friends and family made her feel isolated and alone. It was a feeling that didn't go even after the lockdowns were lifted.

She believed her days in an England shirt were over, even if she wasn't ready for that to be true. Mo was selected for Team GB in the Tokyo Olympics for the summer of 2021 and she played there, losing out to Fiji in the bronze medal match.

Mo focused on media work, commentating for BBC Sport and in the Allianz Premier 15s (now the Premiership Women's Rugby), and coaching provided a welcome distraction. In many ways, her actions were similar to a player edging towards international retirement. In fact, it was on a local radio interview that Mo made her mind up about trying to return to England. The presenter played a clip of Simon Middleton talking about wanting Mo back in the England set-up. 'All she needs to do is put her hand up; we would love to have her back involved,' he said. Mo had not heard the clip before.

After leaving the interview, Mo picked up her phone and texted Simon to say it would be an honour to play again, letting him know she was in a good headspace and that the break had worked well for her.

Middleton met Mo for a chat and told her he thought she still had plenty to offer. Mo's hopes were not up, but then Simon rang her to tell her she was being named in the 2022 Women's Six Nations squad. It was a moment she feels she will never forget.

During that Six Nations, she performed well with four try assists. She was the first-choice scrum half for the World Cup warm-up match against the USA in September, one month from when the team would fly to New Zealand, and was on the bench for the warm-up match against Wales.

Mo completely expected to be picked by Simon Middleton. So confident, in fact, that she had booked in to have her hair coloured and cut, by her hairdresser, the same woman who has done her hair for many years, ready for the flight to New Zealand and the long trip over there.

Mo found out from a phone call with Simon that she would not be going to New Zealand. The shock was so great, she did not know how to deal with the news. In many ways, she still doesn't. She texted her best friend Emily Scarratt, and Sarah Hunter too, and then switched off her phone. Mo lives with Tatyana Heard, the England centre who was called up to the squad, and Bethan Lewis, a Wales player who had also made the World Cup squad. She was in the most uncomfortable position, completely heartbroken, trying to be happy for her friends both in the England squad and those at home.

The rest of the evening is a blur, fuelled by alcohol and tears. Mo isn't a heavy drinker but felt the need to drink, and drink, and drink some more, in order to dampen the pain in her heart. She did not want to go to sleep because she was so scared of waking up and having to process the news all over again.

Players who have not been picked describe the feeling like grief, and that is a word that Helen Davis, the England team's psychologist from October 2021 to July 2023, also uses. Their lives have been put on hold for so many years and there is a sense of loss for the countless sacrifices that have been made in order to play for England. Birthday cakes passed on because of a tailored nutrition plan, nights out refused, pregnancies delayed, family time sacrificed, injuries sustained. All for, in that moment, to lose out on everything.

The pain is felt by all players, but heading into this World Cup where England were predicted to come away with a World Cup trophy was particularly hard to bear. They had been in camp, helping others improve and working as a team, for three months, not counting the five years of preparation for this one tournament. For all that time spent away from home, their lives had only one singular focus: to get to the Rugby World Cup. For those not selected, they would not get the trip to New Zealand with their team, no opportunity to perform on the biggest stage women's rugby had ever seen, and no chance to come home with a Rugby World Cup medal.

'A lot of people say the disappointment of that is almost like a grief process,' Helen explains. 'It's like a grief response, like when someone has died; you go through those stages like disbelief and sadness. And if you look at what that grief response is, you have a big dip and then it's gradually a process of rising out of it. In rugby, the World Cup will be over, but there is another tournament on the horizon [the Six Nations]. And in that tournament those players will see a huge amount of support to get them back into a routine that gets them doing the things they are used to doing in a hugely supportive environment.'

Mo turned up to her hair appointment at 9 a.m. the day after finding out she had not made the squad, walking in with a can of booze on the go, feeling completely numb. She was crying her eyes out, to the point that her hairdresser Jess, whom she had known for many years, got her a huge bouquet of flowers.

Sarah Hunter came down at the weekend that followed to take her crestfallen friend out for breakfast. As they were eating, Mo noticed two missed calls from her mum. Her sister texted Mo telling her she needed to pick up the phone. So when her mum called once more, Mo answered it and her mum said, "Have you seen the article?" The BBC had released the news, before selection had been publicly announced, that she had not made the squad. At that point only Mo's family and the squad knew, which had given her some time to process the news with those closest to her. But now the news was public and Mo couldn't escape the texts or the social media debate about whether it was a good decision or not. At that moment, she hadn't eaten in a few days, and was expecting to debrief with Sarah over a filling breakfast, and instead she broke down in tears once more. She hadn't even told her wider family and the news was no longer for her to share.

What makes it so much harder is how happy Mo was for her team-mates and friends. Lucy Packer, the young and less experienced scrum half, was the one who had been picked in her place. And for Lucy, who was 22 at the time of the Rugby World Cup, the pain was different. She had the joy of being selected for the World Cup, yet was being criticised on social media as if she had stolen the spot from Mo. The more senior of the pair, Mo reached out and offered her support immediately, but she had no capacity to do more than send a text. In those days, it felt like her whole life was over, and her most painful moment was being broadcasted around the world.

Months after the Rugby World Cup, the shock was still so raw, and Mo believes it was an unfair way to be treated. Sarah Hunter said to her that it should never be this much of a shock, and Mo agrees. There were no warning signs that this would happen, Mo says, and she had real hope of being selected. She questions whether her assumption of selection was arrogant, but was pleasantly surprised to realise that team-mates, the media and the rugby-watching public overwhelmingly were shocked by the news.

It's a tough thing to manage for the players selected, too. Mo is best friends with Emily Scarratt, and they have been room-mates with England for years, describing each other as their 'safety blankets' who 'never get bored' of each other. They talk every day, except for at the World Cup. Mo found it too painful to be in contact with Emily other than exchanging a few texts and memes. Her support network was in a different time zone, having a wonderful time at the Rugby World Cup, and Mo was at home, pleased for them but in the same breath absolutely heartbroken for herself.

It's not just the player not selected that the news affects. 'From that moment, I knew England weren't going to win the World Cup,' said Gary Street, the England World Cup-winning coach from 2014. 'And it wasn't as much that he [Simon] didn't pick Mo, but how it affected Scaz. Scaz didn't look like Scaz at the World Cup. And before the World Cup, all of her friends are going: "God, if you can do that to Mo, you can do it to me, and maybe when he said that to me, maybe he was lying about that as well.'"

'I was obviously absolutely gutted for her,' Emily said. 'I suppose part of that is a selfish piece of me. She's my best friend and she's not going to be there, doing one of the toughest things, where inevitably having a good support network around you is obviously going to be more helpful than having them on the other side of the world.

'My reaction [to being selected] was very affected by Mo's news. I was just gutted, and I was physically affected, which isn't a normal thing for me. I'm not really a crier. But that did hit me really hard. It's meant to be a night when you're celebrating with everyone, but it just wasn't right for me to do that because of how close we are. It sounds really dramatic, doesn't it? It's just sport selection, but it means so much.'

Then there was open-side flanker Sadia Kabeya. The young forward, who was only 20 years old at the time of the World Cup, was in fierce competition for the number seven shirt with Marlie Packer and Vicky Fleetwood. In the autumn of 2021, a year before the tournament, Sadia had proved herself with a particularly impressive performance against Canada, which the Red Roses won 51–12. Her work at the breakdown, and being able to turn over the ball well, particularly impressed Simon. Over the next year, Sadia worked on her technical skills under the leadership of Simon and knew heading into the selection stage that she had a good chance of being in the squad. With only four caps before the World Cup, she wondered whether Simon might choose to turn to Vicky instead, who won the World Cup in 2014 and had been on good form for Saracens and England.

The players had the option of how they would like to

know if they hadn't been selected, with options including a phone call, text or email. Sadia asked if she could be texted by Simon if she had not been successful. On the day that the selection would be revealed, Sadia knew the text would come any time in the afternoon before the official announcement at 7 p.m., but she was so nervous that instead of waiting for a text, she decided to put her phone on aeroplane mode until the squad was announced at 7 p.m. At 7.02 p.m., in her lounge with only her house-mate Maya, Sadia decided to take her phone off aeroplane mode and her phone pinged with the sound of lots of messages flooding her notifications. She focused on trying to open the group chat which had the team selection, but her peripheral focus was looking out for the notification of a text from Simon.

As she opened the group chat, there it was. Her name was on the list and Sadia sank into her sofa, unable to process that she was going to a World Cup. Happy tears flowed and she began making the calls to family and friends to share the good news. The relief was overwhelming and the excitement could finally take over.

For Harriet Martin, the team manager, the best moment is when all the selected players arrive at the airport. Not only because somewhere in the back of her mind she was relieved that nobody would miss the flight, but because there were only happy, excited faces around. The whole summer had been full of trepidation and nerves. Players were fighting for their place in the squad and the atmosphere was tense. Now, Harriet was surrounded by beaming smiles and excited players ready to go to New Zealand, hugging their parents and partners as they prepared to go through security. As harsh as it was for the players being left at home, there was no longer a need to tiptoe around fragile emotions. Everyone in that departure terminal was proud and happy. The fun could finally begin.

The team arrived in a jubilant New Zealand, and although there were frosty moods towards the Red Roses from New Zealand fans, there was also a deep respect. The celebrations before the tournament are always fun. The opening ceremony is full of promise and players from all teams can mingle and catch up before the tensions rise.

For Sadia, she felt like a 'competition winner' as she arrived in New Zealand. This is what she had dreamt of from the moment she picked up a rugby ball. But the travel had been exhausting and ahead of the opening round, she went to bed early one night feeling a bit run-down from jet lag. She took her routine Covid-19 test and fell asleep before she could look at the result. In the middle of the night she woke up in a full sweat, aching and feeling really poorly. She turned on her bedside lamp and saw two bold lines on her Covid test, indicating that she had tested positive for the virus. Her heart sank. She texted the team doctor who immediately told her to stay in her room. The next morning, Sadia was moved to a room on her own for five days of isolation. In the darker moments, she thought her dream of playing at the World Cup had been taken from her. She decided to funnel all her energy into staying as fit and healthy as possible, spending a lot of time on her exercise bike, doing workouts with her dumb-bells, and sleeping as much as she could. Food was provided for her in her room, and while players were texting and calling her to make her feel less lonely, she stayed in the room on her own for the full five days.

Before she had gone into isolation, Simon had sat down with her, like he did with every player, to explain what he wanted out of her at the World Cup, and how often she could expect to play. Just before her positive test result, Simon had told Sadia to expect a good amount of game time, and that he was hoping she would start in the first match against Fiji. But after a few days of isolation, Sadia believed all hopes of that had been dashed. Then the team sheet was announced, and once again Sadia was shocked to see her name. She was starting, given the number seven shirt in place of Marlie. By that point, she was feeling better and able to focus on the match that weekend, but had missed out on training sessions and discussions about the game plan.

It made her even more nervous than she already was. Leaving isolation was wonderful, she recalls, but made the significance of the upcoming weekend even more real to her. It was only when she was lining up to sing the national anthem in front of a record Eden Park crowd that her emotions caught up with her. Days before she had been completely isolated in her hotel room, but here she was, singing the national anthem and about to start in her first World Cup match.

In anticipation of their opening game, the coaching staff faced a unique challenge. Because of the disparity in experience between England and Fiji, the staff had limited access to footage of the Fiji women's team in action. The side had played only 18 on-record Test matches in their history before the World Cup which significantly limited how much footage was available of current players.

The Red Roses managed to obtain recordings of two of

Fiji's preparation games. The issue was, they played two very different styles of play in both games, which made trying to analyse them incredibly difficult. In one of the matches, Fiji had adopted a free-flowing, expansive style in which they offloaded the ball frequently. It's an exhausting style of rugby to play but is often only effective for the first half of a match. In the second half, when fatigue creeps in and opponents' superior fitness carries them through. In the other game, Fiji had kept possession of the ball more and tried to play more attritional rugby, which did not suit them as much.

It was clear to the England coaching staff that Fiji's game plan would be focused on playing an offloading game, but replicating such a style in training was not possible for the England players, who were not suited to be able to accurately imitate Fiji's style. It's less skilful and goes against the core principles of England's structured game plan.

The coaching staff recognised they were facing the unknown, although they felt confident that they would win. The preparation camps had been intense and the team were in no doubt of their game plan. With the limited information available, the England coaches focused on reinforcing the team's defensive structures and discipline to counter Fiji's offloading game, while also redeploying key messages about the team's own attacking game plan.

What followed was described by one member of the coaching staff, who didn't want the following comment attributed to him as an 'Oh, shit' or a 'bollocks' (he used both words) moment. The match caught England totally by surprise. It was not the scene-setting, faultless start England had hoped for. The Red Roses looked out of shape for much of the first half as the inevitable nerves of playing on the world stage kicked in. Balls fell loose, penalties were lost, and after 12 minutes, Fiji found themselves over the try line but Zoe Harrison held up the ball. The warning bells were well and truly ringing for England in the first minute as Fiji's No 8 Karalaini Naisewa made a break and ran for 20 metres before finally being taken down.

In the crowd, no doubt, were Black Ferns fans thinking, 'Bring on the final.' It was the wake-up call England needed to regather their discipline and shape. Amy Cokayne, the England hooker, ran over for England's second try, from a lineout and driving maul, and Abbie Ward followed her shortly afterwards, pushed over the try line by Sarah Bern. It was a double blow for Fiji who lost their captain, Sereima Leweniqila, to the sin bin for pulling down a maul on the build-up to Abbie's try.

By half-time, only ten points separated a team who had been fully professional for three and a half years, and one that remained entirely amateur. England had conceded two tries, half the number they conceded throughout their entire Women's Six Nations campaign earlier that year.

The second half was a different game as England pulled away with better fitness, a stronger bench and a perilous attacking maul. 'We changed tactically at half-time,' Louis Deacon explains. 'Before the game we felt that if we played fast with a high ball-in-play time that would suit us, but it didn't. It actually suits Fiji's style of play, because of their sevens background, and how they like to play – loose and quite unstructured. So at half-time I remember actually standing up and saying we've got to make the game really structured. So we'll go to our set piece to tie them in and that will free up the space. The second half was a completely different story.'

Fiji lost their power and could not keep up. There was no shortness of passion from Fiji, who fought until the end, but they were outclassed by England. Amy opened the second-half scoring with her second try, after carrying the ball ten metres at the back of the maul, and Zoe Aldcroft soon followed her across the whitewash, spotting a gap in the Fiji defence. The floodgates had opened.

Lydia Thompson crossed twice in three minutes before she cleared the way for the remarkable return of Abby Dow, the England winger who broke her leg against Wales in the Six Nations earlier that year. Abby's leg twisted so horrifically in a tackle that the break was described as 'lengthways' by a doctor, affecting the top and bottom of her leg. As chapter four described, a team gathered around Abby, of physiotherapists, surgeons, doctors and coaches to form a plan to get her back on the pitch for this exact moment. She undertook intense rehabilitation and six months later, she had taken off her bib, had done her warm-up exercises, and ran on to the pitch to a roar of support from fans in the whole stadium – regardless of their loyalties. This was a moment that everyone could relate to.

Within minutes, Abby scored a trademark try: an aggressive run down the touchline, just four minutes upon her return to rugby. How England had missed her. Yet with six tries in the first 20 minutes of the second half from the Red Roses, you might have thought they hadn't suffered for her absence.

England confirmed their sheer class with three further second-half tries from Claudia MacDonald, four in total for the winger, one from scrum half Leanne Infante, and a final one for replacement hooker Connie Powell to bow out England's record-breaking win. A consolation try on 80 minutes from Fiji's scrum half Lavena Cavuru was well deserved for the competitive first half the debutants, ranked 12th in the world, offered.

It was England's 26th win in a row, a record-setting win for the team, yet there was a sense of unease in the performance. In a week's time they would face France, their closest Six Nations rivals, and second closest rivals to New Zealand, whose much tighter defence and stronger fitness could put a stop to the rampant England attack.

The match was full of faults but Sadia Kabeya was the star of the show. Her ruthless approach to the breakdown secured her a player of the match performance, completing a successful return from isolation. It felt like a full-circle moment for the flanker, who just a week before the match believed her World Cup dreams had been shattered before they had begun.

England's first real test of the tournament came in the second week against France. Both teams were fairly confident of finishing in the top two of Pool C, which would see them go through to the knockout stages, but England knew that beating France would extend their unbeaten run to 27 Tests and secure their place in the quarter-finals, but finishing top of their pool would give them an easier run-up to the final.

It was a brutal match which saw France lose two stars, scrum half Laure Sansus and No 8 Romane Ménager, in the first quarter. Towards the end of the match, with France within one score of England in the final ten minutes, those absences arguably carried England to the win. It was a reminder of just how tight margins can be at the top of the game. Sarah Hunter described the match as 'attritional', and a few scuffles between the teams illustrated just how heated the contest was between the two sides.

Emily Scarratt scored all England's points in the 13–7 win, including a first-half try and penalty to give the Red Roses a bit of breathing space at half-time. Her try was the result of a 14-phase move which ended with fly half Zoe Harrison popping a pass to Emily, who used her height advantage to reach over French players to dot the ball down.

Back in England, fans had gathered for the first official watch party for the Rugby World Cup. In a packed-out bar in Victoria, London, fans were watching the rugby from 7 a.m., thanks to the time difference. A new rule was started: the time it is appropriate to drink is based on the time in New Zealand, not the time in England, and the bar staff said it was the earliest they had ever had to change a Guinness barrel. Like so many other times during the World Cup, that watch party felt like a significant moment. At least, it felt like a big change in the consumption of women's rugby. There were more people crammed into that pub at 7 a.m. on a cold, dark October morning than there had been at some of the Red Roses' first international games.

In the pub were former Red Roses, journalists, content creators and lots of women's rugby fans. Some were more sober than others by the second half, but the atmosphere was wonderful. Children had dragged their parents out of bed at 5 a.m. to get to the event and proudly wore Red Roses shirts which looked more like dresses on their tiny bodies. One child there had odd shoes on because daddy had dressed her in the dark that morning. We have a chat and she tells me that when she grows up she wants to be Jess Breach. Not an England rugby player, no, she actually wants to *be* Jess Breach, for two reasons, which she counts on her fingers to help me keep up: one, Jess is fast, and two, Jess is pretty.

It occurs to me that as a child I had no female role models in sport at all. They existed, but I didn't know anything about them. Yet this girl, in her Red Roses dress, butterfly-patterned tights and mismatched shoes, will know no different than always having accessible strong role models to aspire to be. As this young girl grows up, she will realise that Jess is more than just fast and pretty. She is also a kind person with lots of friends, intelligent, hugely switched on to business and the media, and has overcome personal tragedy with great courage. The little girl had the same adoration in her eyes for Jess that I had for Fizz from *Tweenies*. But her role model is a real woman, who speaks up about body image and real issues that affect her. 'Can't see it, can't be it' is essentially the slogan of women's rugby these days, but at that watch party I saw first-hand the impact the team was having on that young generation.

The second half was just as brutal as the first. England maintained the bulk of possession but it switched regularly and both teams seemed more defensive than attacking. It was a bruising match which players recall as being one of the toughest matches they had ever played.

Tactically, whatever France did, England followed, and whatever England did, France followed. As bodies grew more tired towards the end of the second half, France opted to kick the ball more, and deeper, to put pressure on the backfield, so England did the same. Whereas the ball seemed to move only inches each phase in the first half, it was suddenly spending more time in the air than in hands. The margin between these two sides was small, but France's solid defence was to be marvelled. They made 227 tackles to England's 73, with a higher success rate than England despite having three times as many tackles to make. They held England as close as they could. England carried the ball for 449 metres, more than double France's total, and had 70 per cent of the possession, yet only mustered one try.

England's problems with finishing had been exposed, bodies were battered, but the goal had been achieved. Next up was South Africa, a semi-professional side whom England were expected to storm past.

Simon made 15 changes to his 23-player squad that faced France in the previous week, to give opportunities to more players in his squad to step up, and even decided to rest Sarah Hunter, the oldest player in the England team whose body needed a rest after the tight wrestle with France.

For the players that had been selected, this was a huge opportunity to show what they were capable of, and they took full advantage of it. England's show-stopping 75–0 win was dominated by their ruthless set piece, the imperious driving maul granting eight of England's 13 tries. Twelve of the side's tries were scored by forwards, including six that were scored directly from the maul and two in which a driving maul was used in the build-up to the try.

But issues with passing errors in the first half had stifled England's attack and a more expansive play wasn't rewarding England. The team put their faith in the Tank and rolled on, perilous in their drive.

While the back line struggled at times with cohesion, spilling the ball in contact regularly, there were moments of wonder from centre Tatyana Heard, who was instrumental in England's attack. Her crashing runs or well-timed passes carried England in the second half especially, giving the forwards space to play in with front-foot ball. After the hour mark, three tries came in four minutes, from Poppy Cleall, Sadia Kabeya and Abby Dow, and Tatyana had played her role in orchestrating each one.

Both Rosie Galligan, in the second row, and Connie Powell, hooker, recorded hat-tricks, the former in particularly high spirits after the match after a near-perfect performance. Just three years before the World Cup, Rosie had been rushed to hospital after contracting meningitis, and doctors warned her that had she sought medical help only a day later, she could have lost both of her legs. As she ran to cross the try line four times (the fourth try ruled out by TMO), nobody smiled as much as Rosie, and nobody cheered as loudly in the crowd as parents Holly and Tim. Rosie's fine performance was testament to the sheer strength in depth of the Red Roses squad because despite a near-perfect game for the second row, Rosie was unlikely to take a starting shirt off Abbie Ward, England's finest lineout technician, or Zoe Aldcroft, who the year before had won World Rugby's player of the year accolade, in the knockout stages of the tournament.

Fittingly, England women's football manager Sarina Wiegman was in the crowd. 'We've talked a lot about the Lionesses, particularly as a coaching group and how they went about creating that winning environment, and how you transfer it into a winning tournament environment,' Simon said after the match. 'We've certainly learned some things from what they did and I think they showed great adaptability and resilience in the Euros. We've had to do that sometimes and we have done.'

A clean sheet and 13 tries against the Springboks gave England a perfect springboard into the knockout stages, but concerns over their ability to hold on to the ball under pressure remained. In the pool stages, England had scored 172 points and conceded only 26, yet that statistic masked concerns about the performances. On the surface, England appeared untouchable, but greater challenges lay ahead.

Off the pitch, the team tried to find ways of having fun that didn't involve rugby, and Simon had the perfect idea. He loves fishing and wanted to try and catch some red snappers, large pink fish that are known to be delicious. So he commandeered a boat and invited players and staff to join him. Red Roses fishing for red snappers.

'We got a fishing boat and went out to do some sea fishing. It was really cool and nice to do something completely different,' Emily Scarratt remembers. 'None of us are fishing people except for Midds, who wasn't actually that good. It was quite funny.' From the staff, Scott and Louis said yes, as did Liam Staines, the video producer, and Calum the analyst joined in too. Hannah Botterman, Emily, Laura Keates and Abbie all decided to go as well. Simon was excited to show the players another side to him, but it turns out Abbie is the queen of both England's lineout and the fishing line, and her catch was the biggest of the day. Nobody's smile was bigger than Simon's, as the team pulled into a cove and barbecued some of the fish they had caught and ate it for lunch. 'Obviously, hanging out with some of the male staff on a different level to what you're used to was really nice,' Emily said. 'I think with trips like that, you get to see the chilled, social versions of the coaches, whereas so often they're just 'Coach Midds' or 'Coach Deacs', and they kind of take on that different role. It definitely makes you feel like you know them more as a person.'

England could be comfortably confident heading into their quarter-final with Australia. The Red Roses were on the back of a 28-match winning streak and had won all five of their previous encounters with Australia by at least ten points.

Before the quarter-final match against Australia, severe weather warnings were put into place across New Zealand and the match was at serious risk of being called off. The conditions were horrendous. Rachael Burford, who was commentating on the match, said they were the worst she had ever seen and Robert Kitson, the *Guardian* journalist commented: 'The first half might have been slightly drier for all involved had it taken place in a car wash.' The pitch was covered in standing pools of water and there were splashes of water every time a boot hit the pitch, making running difficult and legs heavier.

In preparation, Simon spoke to the Thorns (the team's senior leadership group) and the strategy group to make sure everyone was aware that if the game was called off at half-time, as seemed increasingly likely as the first half played out, the result would stand. That meant players should look to do all they could to be ahead at half-time, and Emily Scarratt, the team's most experienced kicker, should opt to kick for the posts whenever a good opportunity presented itself. And the rest of the game plan? Do whatever is humanly possible to win that match in terrible conditions.

The monsoonal weather was so extreme that it felt unsafe at times, especially in rucks, as pools of water gathered on the floor. At one point in the first half, Marlie Packer handed off an Australian player who fell backwards and slid three feet on the floor. Players were slipping and sliding across the pitch and falling in tackles. England reverted to a close-range game that focused on keeping the ball in hand as much as possible, aware that a slippery ball would not travel too well with long passes to the wings. Kicks were distorted in the wind, so the ball was better off kept in hand. 'I honestly thought the first time the referee went to TMO, as she called time off I thought she was going to call off the game,' Emily Scarratt remembers.

Just before half-time, the clocks in the UK went back by an hour, lending the bizarre situation of the end of the first half being played before the kick-off time. 'Australia wish they could have turned back the clocks after that first-half performance,' I penned for *The Times*, before a wiser editor told me to stop my nonsense.

England led 19–5 at half-time, and as the players jogged back to the changing rooms, their kit truly soaked through, they wondered if they would play the second half. Harriet gave players the option of a fresh kit if they wanted to get changed and many took up the offer of being momentarily dry and warm, before they were soaked again in the second half. Emily decided that changing into a dry kit would be pointless, but she did wring out her socks, and was shocked at the amount of water that poured out of those and her boots.

The rain stopped towards the end of the second half, but it didn't give England enough time to practise a more expansive style of rugby. They played to their super strength of the set piece, the lineout driving maul, and it led to the criticisms explored in the previous chapter. The reality was, England had no choice in this game than to play to the strongest part of their plan: keep the ball close, and use sheer power to cross the whitewash. Knockout rugby doesn't need to be beautiful, but it must be effective. All seven of England's tries came from the pack.

'A lot has been said about the driving maul and how we're scoring tries,' Sarah Hunter said after the match. 'But, ultimately, no one's going to look back and go, "Oh, how did England score?"

'They look at the result and if it isn't broke you don't need to fix it. I don't think there's any concerns within ourselves about how we want to play or what we're doing at the minute. If it's not working, we know we've got other things to go to.'

Simon matched Sarah's words: 'Rugby doesn't have to be play, play, play and shift, shift, shift. That's southern hemisphere rugby – fantastic. We're a northern hemisphere side. We're very good at what we do, they're very good at what they do. You play to your strengths and I don't really recognise the criticism.'

Had the match been in drier conditions, Australia would have offered a fine test of England's play-making backs, had England opted to roll out a more free-flowing style of play. At that point in the tournament, comments made by coaches hinted that the Red Roses had another style of play hidden up their sleeve, ready to whip out in the final. Near the end of the already-won quarter-final would have been a good time to test that mode of rugby under pressure from top-level opponents, which would have been useful preparation for New Zealand, but it wasn't to be. That style stayed under wraps and on powered the Tank, straight over Australia's semi-final hopes.

The match was special for another, very important, reason. Captain Sarah, a try scorer on the day, finished the game as the most capped England international of all time with her 138th appearance for the Red Roses. Sarah's contribution to the Red Roses is exemplary. Simon notes that he has never seen her have a bad training day, and players are full of praise for the 'ultimate leader'. She is England Rugby's greatest servant and was fittingly awarded a CBE by King Charles III in his 2023 birthday honours.

'Sarah is the most honest and professional player I have ever known let alone worked with,' Simon said when asked to describe his skipper. 'Throughout her career her commitment to being the best version of herself at every opportunity has shone through in her attention to detail and faultless preparation.

'I'd say she has maximised every ounce of her potential, which if when you reflect on your career you can say that, then it puts you in a very special category.

'She's an absolute inspiration for everybody who has played with her or worked with her and is the ultimate example to every young person who would want to play. The word legend is overused but it's most definitely not in her case; she is and will always be a true England legend.'

Sarah and the team were in high spirits after a good run of matches which had set up a semi-final against Canada. But before that, there was some important business to attend to. The day after the quarter-final was Halloween, and social secretary Sarah McKenna pulled out all the stops to make it an event to remember for the Red Roses. Sarah is Captain Fun in the squad. She loves a practical joke and some estimate that she spent more money in a joke shop in New Zealand than she earned in the tournament. Fake spiders are a classic Sarah move, but organising elaborate events are her favourite parts of tournaments. 'You've got to have a laugh,' she says, reflecting on the tournament. 'It can be such a stressful time so I like doing stuff to make the girls remember that it's fun too.'

There's a healthy pinch of the old school about Sarah, who enjoys the off-pitch side of rugby camp life a lot and takes her role as unofficial social sec very seriously. There's often a smirk on her face and a look of mischief in her eyes. 'You can't underestimate the importance of having some-one like McKenna in the squad,' former Red Rose Rachael Burford says, laughing as she clearly remembers some of the daft things Sarah would do to make her team-mates smile.

At the World Cup, in preparation for Halloween night, Sarah had visited the joke shop and bought props to help her decorate the team room, and a corridor that led to the team room. She had hired actors (well, team-mates includ-ing Jess Breach) to jump out at players as they tried to enter the room, and she had organised snacks and a horror film for the team to watch. Never scared to get involved, Sarah zipped herself up in a suitcase and kicked her legs to scare team-mates walking by. It worked. Whereas most of the Red Roses found it a fun night, poor Maud Muir found the whole thing particularly frightening. Maud is not one for horror films at the best of times, but the fright of players jumping out at her was enough to make her cry and need ten minutes to recover from all the action. 'I was having a rough day anyway,' Maud says, smiling, but clearly a bit defensive about the reports of her being scared. 'I was emotionally not stable at that point anyway, and then it didn't help that I got really terrified.' She emphasises the 'really' in that sentence, to stress the point that it would have scared anyone.

Earlier in the tournament, Sarah had organised a Greek night for the squad, which involved the team eating Greek food and taking part in traditional Greek activities. Reader, if you are not already doing so, please imagine Harriet Martin's face when Sarah came to her with the suggestion. Once more, Sarah was in town buying props for her idea. She wanted to smash plates, a classic Greek tradition, but aware that Harriet might have something to say about that, she opted to bulk-buy some paper plates instead. And so she stood on her chair, throwing paper plates on the floor.

The pinnacle of the night was a team flash mob. Sarah started it, of course, and then players were supposed to jump up on to their chairs around the room and also start dancing. The problem was, other players had forgotten their cue, or were too distracted to notice Sarah on her chair, so she was performing on her own. Thankfully for Sarah, Marlie (who was oblivious to plans for a flash mob) will never miss an opportunity to dance, so from the other side of the room she stood up and started dancing too. Others then joined in and after a while, the whole squad was on their feet dancing to Greek music.

'Everyone hates forced fun,' Maud says, and there can be quite a few team-bonding activities organised that the players roll their eyes to, especially when it's accompanied by a camera crew ready to plaster the 'fun' all over social media.

'But it isn't forced when you're actually having a good time as well. It was very important just to get away from rugby for a bit and be a bit normal. I love that sort of stuff. Some people hate it, but I really enjoy it.'

As the semi-final approached, the media in England were speculating that the team were too reliant on the maul, and word of the coverage seeped into the Red Roses camp. The success of the team was at this point unrivalled – no team in men's or women's rugby had ever won 28 games in a row, and to the team, the criticism of how they got there felt like nit-picking. 'I think the higher you go, the more people want to knock you off and unfortunately, I think specifically with women, we're not very good at hyping each other up and instead the first thing we do is knock each other down,' Sarah Bern told me, as she prepared for the match. I agreed with her, and while it's often worse for women, I point out that Marcus Smith, the England and Harlequins fly half, had been billed as the next greatest rugby player of all time and when he failed to reach that pinnacle in every game, he was criticised harshly.

'It's just a society thing,' Sarah replies. 'I think people have watched us play previously and expect us to just run away with games and score fantastic tries that go viral, but that's not always the case. Every team and every player is trying to be the best they can be at this tournament so it's going to come down to who can be the fittest, make the most tackles, make the least mistakes. We do get a lot of criticism, because we have high expectations, but I think that's just a result of society.'

The team were not used to such criticism, but they were fair in their belief that the attention was too focused on their maul. The tournament had felt like England's to lose and while there was plenty of coverage about just how excellent the team were, when a team is considered 'perfect' there is the temptation to look for their Achilles heel or to speculate which team possesses the kryptonite to take them down. After England vs South Africa, the post-match analysis was so damning you might have thought England had lost 75–0, rather than won it by such a scoreline. The team were held to impossibly high standards, so much that a simple knock-on would find itself in match reports as journalists looked for any glimpse that this team was fallible.

'We have a huge target on our backs so we know we just have to keep our heads down, stick together and keep pushing down those tough times,' Sarah said. 'People put Emily Scarratt on this huge pedestal and say she's a perfect player. I mean, we're still human. We're not just rugby players and we still make mistakes; we have off days. Sometimes people need to remember that. People will say they are 'uncharacteristic mistakes', but sometimes it's just how you turn up on the day and just your stars aren't aligning, but it's nothing to do with your effort or you as a player.'

England brushed the criticism aside when they faced Canada in the semi-final, but they didn't take long to remind fans that they would not be changing their strategy. In the seventh minute Marlie crossed over in classic Marlie style, a lineout driving maul from close range. Next came a moment of excellent carrying from Helena Rowland whose delayed pass to Abby Dow allowed the winger to cross for her first of the match. Canada played England at their own game, and twice the English side of the maul collapsed against Canada's strong forward pack.

The try of the tournament and World Rugby's women's try of the year came in the second half, from Abby Dow. But really it came from Claudia MacDonald. And really it began four years before that match, when Abby and Claudia were at Wasps together. As contracts were in their infancy back then, Abby and Claudia spent their days on the pitch at Wasps, in West London, doing skills training. One of the moves they trained was a long swooping pass from Claudia, who played as a scrum half at the time, that Abby would gather mid-run on the wing, and finish the move with a sprint to the try line. They practised and practised, week in and week out, but they never used it in a game. Without planning it, they had saved the move for a crucial moment in the semi-final of the Rugby World Cup.

England were pinned behind their own try line, with Canada's physiotherapists still on the pitch, when Claudia decided to run with the ball. She beat seven defenders on her run, starting on the left wing and ending in the centre of the pitch. She looked to her right and spotted Abby out on the opposite wing, waving at her to remind her of those training days at Wasps. It's one thing to land a 20-metre pass while standing still and a very different thing to land such a risky pass in a high-pressure environment – closer to their own try line than the opposition's – and at speed. Claudia looped a perfectly weighted cross-field pass that landed in the basket of Abby's arms and the race was on. With Ellie Kildunne behind her with supportive screams of 'Go Abby, yes Abby!' she sprinted from the 22-metre line all the way to the goal line and scored.

'When Claudia gave me that ball I was like, "Right, we can finish this," Abby said after the match. 'I just decided to run as hard as I could. It was an absolute team effort to begin with, though. We were on our line and managed to shift it and turn it into a great attack.'

The match was nail-bitingly close in the final 20 minutes as Canada became only the second team to get within 25 points of England during the Red Roses' 30-match winning streak, the other being France. Emily Scarratt closed the scoring with a penalty in the 70th minute that padded out England's lead to seven points. Almost immediately afterwards, Canada's attack once more threatened England and built 20 phases of play before Ellie Kildunne ripped the ball out of their grasp. England held on to possession as much as possible, under pressure constantly, before Zoe Harrison nudged the ball out of play to end a classic World Cup match with England ahead 26–19.

Canada had almost matched England's forward dominance and they tested every inch of England's nerve, often holding them still in the maul or pushing them backwards. In a match that ended with just a seven-point lead to England, a professional team, against Canada, an amateur team, the Red Roses had to concede that they had not played their best game. 'We know we weren't anywhere near our best today but Canada didn't let us be anywhere near our best,' said Simon after the match. 'I thought we got a little bit tight. We had a great first 15 minutes and then we just let Canada in, and it made us nervous. It's understandable. The pressure on this team is huge, as we know. The expectation is massive on these girls, yet they keep delivering time and time again. We found a way to win and that's the most important thing.

'If we'd had an easy semi-final and got through it, we

wouldn't have been ready for next week,' he said. 'We'll be ready for next week now.'

In the build-up to the World Cup, England players were further incentivised to win by performance-related bonuses. If they progressed out of the pool stage, they would receive a £2,500 bonus, and a further £2,500 if they reached the final. If the team took home the World Cup, they would pocket a further £10,000 – for a grand total of £15,000 per player. The total bonus pool for the entire team was £480,000, less than 10 per cent of the £5 million bonus pot, with an extra £1 million for coaches and management, promised to the England's men's team if they won the 2019 Rugby World Cup.

As England had stormed towards the final, so too had New Zealand, who as the tournament's home team had benefited from great support from the crowds. And while the tournament looked like a celebration of the Black Ferns, it masked how underfunded and undersupported the players really were. New Zealand were not due to receive any bonus for winning, despite each All Blacks player being awarded NZ$134,000 (more than some of the Black Ferns' yearly salary) for their 2015 World Cup victory.

Off the pitch, New Zealand Rugby had not supported the players as best they could. There was an awkward moment in the run-up to the Black Ferns' quarter-final when their governing body had forgotten about the Women's Rugby World Cup when organising a match between the men's team and Japan at the same time the women faced Wales. In a statement, New Zealand Rugby said: 'Unfortunately, when Japan Rugby set the kick-off time for the All Blacks Test, NZR did not take into account the Rugby World

Cup stipulation that the host nation would play in the quarter-final 2 time slot regardless of pool results and may inadvertently cause a clash.'

The Black Ferns had long been advocating for themselves, not least Ruby Tui, the charismatic, electric winger whose viral post-match speeches and autobiography have captured the spirit of the Black Ferns. Before the final, Ruby set the scene perfectly: 'In 2010 nobody knew who the Black Ferns were. We were told we would never be paid. We were told we'd never play at Eden Park. We were told women's rugby didn't matter. And now here we are 12 years later and Eden Park is sold out, bro. It's a really, really special moment. Kiwis are normally so laid-back we're lying down but we've finally got up.'

In New Zealand's semi-final, France battle-hardened them as much as they had against England in Pool C, but instead of the seven-point lead England held, New Zealand were pinned down for most of the match, unable to release their slippery wingers and cause havoc on the scoreline. Only one point put the Black Ferns in front in the final ten minutes, and when France's Caroline Drouin was granted a penalty with 61 seconds left before the clock turned red, it felt like England would face their most familiar rivals in the final. But the fly half missed, skewing her kick just to the left, in yet another reminder of how important kicking is becoming in women's rugby. The Black Ferns regained possession and held on for just three phases before opting to kick the ball out and secure their place in a home World Cup final. England knew who their opponents would be. It was their oldest rivals.

The final two teams were to be predicted before the tournament, but Canada and France got frighteningly close – a good indicator of just how much women's rugby is developing. England and New Zealand had faced each other in the finals of the 2002, 2006, 2010 and 2017 World Cups, with all those matches won by New Zealand.

The experiences of 2017 were firm in the memories of the nine England players who were lining up to play in the 2021 edition. Sarah Hunter, Marlie Packer, Alex Matthews, Abbie Ward, Sarah Bern, Amy Cokayne, Vickii Cornborough, Emily Scarratt and Lydia Thompson were there with the aim of fixing the heartbreak of the previous tournament. Abbie had carried a photo from that final in her wallet for the past five years, to remind herself of that pain and to motivate her performances.

'As senior players we just wanted to make sure the elephants in the room had been addressed; this isn't just any other game,' Emily said. 'So for people who had never been in that environment before, or been under that much pressure before, we wanted to make sure that if they had any questions they could talk it through and actually be a bit vulnerable. But in the same breath, you also don't want to make it even bigger in their heads. I try to leave that on them as much as possible. The worst thing you can do, as coaches or senior players, is change all of a sudden. People see straight through it and they'll think you're really stressed, so it's about trying to keep things similar.

'And in that week [heading into the World Cup final], I actually carried more baggage than many of the girls. Some of them had never lost in an England shirt, whereas I've lost two finals to New Zealand, that's now three. So potentially my baggage is less helpful to them. I was just trying to be whatever people needed that week to put us in the best possible place for that final.'

One of the most interesting match-ups ahead of the match was on the wing, between Portia Woodman and Lydia Thompson. In the 2017 edition of the World Cup final, the pair had been playing their own game of cat and mouse, tightly matched and highly competitive. Both are powerful in contact and have sizzling pace. Both had a similar job: get the ball, run fast, and step some defenders on the way if you can. And if your opponent is doing the above, try to tackle them.

But the most exciting selection decision for England was Holly Aitchison at inside centre. Holly added another kicking threat to England's back line, which was already star-studded with two of the best kickers in women's rugby: Zoe at fly half and Emily at outside centre. Holly's selection, in place of Tatyana Heard, hinted at how Simon wanted to play. Holly's experience in the sevens game gave her a solid base for the tempo this match would need and her triple threat of kicking, running and passing were the key to unlocking the potential in England's back line, by seeing space in the backfield or using her trademark delayed pass to trick the defence into tackling the wrong player. Holly dances with the ball in hand, never looks under pressure for too long, and rarely misses a beat. Her opponent, Theresa Fitzpatrick, is the queen of offloads and while also a triple threat, her skills were more developed than Holly's.

England's forward pack was expected to be stronger than New Zealand's, but the offloading game of the Black Ferns was a worry for the Red Roses. They hadn't handled that style well against Fiji, and now faced a team much stronger in that style of play, with supreme fitness and handling skills to make the style more punishing.

The team lined up to watch the Black Ferns' Haka, the Ko Ūhia Mai. As the spectacle unfolded, the Red Roses stood two metres or so apart, their hands clasped, faces stern and eye contact held. Rivalries do not come much bigger than this. Referee Hollie Davidson blew her whistle, game on. Renee Holmes kicked the ball into the hands of Lydia Thompson, and the match – tantalising from that first kick – was under way. With two minutes on the clock, England won a lineout and New Zealand assumed the Red Roses would play the ball narrow, rather than shifting to the wings. But England were here to play a more expansive game and the ball shifted from the lineout on the right touchline, all the way to the left touchline, and back to the right again when Ellie Kildunne tapped the ball down in the right-hand corner. With four minutes on the clock, England were 7–0 up.

England were then given a penalty 15 metres out from their try line and the opportunity to test their strongest weapon against their fiercest rivals was too good of an opportunity for the Red Roses to miss. Zoe Harrison kicked the ball out and set up a lineout about seven metres from the try line. Amy Cokayne threw the ball to Abbie Ward, who twisted perfectly in the air to present the ball to the back of the maul, putting the keys firmly in the Tank's ignition. Abbie marshalled her troops with roars of instruction, but the Red Roses were halted in their drive, as the Black Ferns defended it better than any team England had faced up until that point. Eventually Amy crossed, putting England 14–0 ahead.

The Red Roses had an idyllic start to the match. Then, in one blood-curdling moment, everything changed. Lydia ran towards Portia, who was bolting down the touchline and, in a split-second decision, Lydia went too high and hit her opposite number in the head. Portia was unconscious, showing symptoms of brain injury including what appeared to be chronic posturing, her arms sticking up in an unnatural motion. It was awful, unlawful, and that one hit would change the course of the game. Lydia was shown a red card and Portia was out of the game. England had to play for almost three-quarters of the match with 14 players and New Zealand had lost their star winger.

As Lydia walked off the pitch, in shock at what had just happened, it was her close friend Sarah McKenna, on water duty, who walked off with her.

New Zealand had the chance to capitalise on the overlap and almost immediately after the game restarted Georgia Ponsonby scored for New Zealand, followed across the try line shortly afterwards by Woodman's replacement Ayesha Leti-I'iga. The match was end to end and at half-time, England led precariously by 26–19. Within 30 seconds of the second half, Stacey Fluhler crossed over to start an almighty comeback for the Black Ferns. England were facing an onslaught, but until the 48th minute had still been leading for the entire game. Suddenly, England were behind. Sarah Bern won a penalty in the 53rd minute and England opted to kick for the corner and go for the lineout driving maul. At this point, any criticism of the tactic was surely out of the window. In a World Cup final, a win is a win. Abbie marshalled the Tank and Amy Cokayne crossed over for her hat-trick. In the 64th minute, Abby made a run but was hit in the head by Kennedy Simon, the flanker. It was similar to Lydia's hit on Portia, but the referee saw it as a yellow card rather than a red. As a yellow card leaves the player in the sin bin for ten minutes, that meant Kennedy could return for the final five minutes. And just how crucial would those final five minutes prove to be.

With nine minutes to play, New Zealand were in front again and England could not fight their way back. In the dying moments of the game, with the score 34–31 in New Zealand's favour, England were handed a golden chance: a lineout five metres from their try line. This was one last chance to use their Tank. If it's successful, they win the World Cup, if it's unsuccessful, they have lost it. Simon describes it as the highest pressure moment that could ever exist. He turned to Louis and said, 'This is it. We have got one shot to win the World Cup.'

Abbie, the most tactically gifted lineout leader in the world, jumped for the ball but it was well contested by New Zealand who managed to tip it into their control. Before the final whistle had been blown, the Black Ferns were already celebrating on the pitch. Against all odds, England's worst nightmare had been realised. The winning streak was over, in brutal fashion, and the shock hit the England players.

Up in the coaches' box, there was only silence. It wasn't even a head-in-hands moment, there were no swear words being screamed or comforts being spoken. Only silence. Simon made his way to the pitch to console the players. As Eden Park roared at maximum volume and New Zealand players jumped in the air, his eyes darted around, trying to spot Lydia in the furore. She was the first player he wanted to see. 'As soon as the whistle went, she was the first person I wanted to get to because I knew what she'd be thinking,' Simon recalls.

Walking towards her, he was thinking carefully about what to say. No matter what happened, he wanted her to know that losing the final wasn't her fault. No matter how seismic an event her sending-off proved to be, no game can be lost by one player. As he jumped down the steps from the coaches' box, he thought about what she must be thinking in that moment and wanted to let her know that she had his support. Eventually he found Lydia, who was crumpled in her own tears, and he hugged her.

'She said, "I'm so sorry, I'm so sorry," to me, and I said, "Listen, mate, it is part of sport, it's not your fault." There are loads of things that went wrong in that final,' Simon reflects. 'You can't allow players to carry something like that around for the rest of their lives. They're going to do that anyway, but you've got to bring down that sense of letting the team down as far as possible. Abbie was the same and I said to her too, if it wasn't for all the amazing lineouts she got right in the build-up to the final, we probably wouldn't be here. So it's about making them realise that that's the nature of sport. I couldn't be more proud of the team really.'

Then he walked on to the pitch slowly, focused on his players who were in tears on the pitch, many crouching on the floor and others helping console their team-mates. Emily remembers feeling in 'genuine disbelief'. 'Never did I feel like we weren't in control of that game, and I know that sounds daft given what happened, but never did I think we weren't good enough to win it. When that whistle went, it was just . . .' Emily pauses and then exhales loudly. 'My initial thing was just trying to find people that might need you. Everyone is absolutely upset, and you're not going to help anyone in that moment but you're just trying to make sure nobody is by themselves.'

In the corner of Simon's eye, he could see the Black Ferns celebrating with their fans. At that moment, sport's cruel balance was most vivid. The highest highs are always juxtaposed with the lowest lows.

He embraced Holly Aitchison and told her that she did everything she possibly could. He told her to be really proud – nothing else – just really proud. She nodded, but in truth the defeat was felt personally by every England player on the pitch.

'It's a team sport, you're in it together,' Simon said to the players after the match. 'You can't all of a sudden not be in it together because somebody gets something wrong.'

Months after the World Cup, players describe the final as a trauma. It sounds ridiculous to describe losing a final as a traumatic event when there is so much suffering in the world, but that is the word many players use to describe it. And they can be cut some slack for using the word. It's obvious that some players hold the 2021 World Cup as a very personal tragedy. One mention of the final causes tears in many players.

In March 2023, Lydia wrote a piece for women's rugby website *Scrum Queens* about the red card, and how much she suffered in the aftermath:

> When it happened, I felt numb. In that moment, after the red card went up – just totally numb. Initially I was just worried about Portia because of what had happened – the collision of heads – felt quite horrific. My body then went into some sort

of protective shut down which I realised afterwards. I watched the game in the dugout, but I just can't even connect with the person who was watching, because it wasn't me at all.

When the final whistle went, I really did feel broken, and I couldn't stop crying. I just wanted to apologise to my team-mates and to Portia.

It was a sense of relief to see her back on the field at the end of the game, but I felt devastated to have taken the full 80 minutes away from her too. Seeing that she is back playing now and is as awesome as ever, well that is really reassuring and important for me because of course I never step on the field to hurt someone.

When it was over and it sunk in that we'd lost, I felt like it was 100 per cent my fault and I still get those thoughts. I wanted to apologise again and again. People were incredibly kind to me after the game when maybe I was expecting blame and I just couldn't stop crying or take it in. I found my family in the end and just sobbed.

People say – give it time, but you don't believe them when you're in a bad place. I know this sounds stupid, but for a while after the final, I couldn't even imagine laughing again – that is how I felt, the idea of even having a normal conversation just felt impossible.

I came back and just decided to withdraw a bit and simplify my life. I came off social media – though I wasn't very good at it anyway – and for a while I went back working for my family's manufacturing business just because I didn't want to be at home. Waking up and having a straight-forward routine really helped – I went to work, had a good lunch, sat in an office, did my tasks and that was huge.

I started to think, well I am going to have to live with all these thoughts, so I need to start engaging a bit more with people.

Lydia spoke to a clinical psychologist, whom she had worked with before the World Cup, to help her come to terms with the incident.

Perhaps the trauma comes from the shock. England were sure favourites. People were calling the whole tournament a dead rubber before it had begun. And it would have been the perfect fairytale for England. Thirty-one games unbeaten, winning the World Cup against their closest rivals after the heartbreak of 2017, in front of a world-record (at the time) crowd of 42,579 fans.

There were tears in the changing room as players had to continue their duties: Maud was in the anti-doping room, as players are picked randomly for drug testing after matches, and Emily, Abbie, Sarah Bern and others were called to do media duty. They had 20 minutes to have a shower and compose themselves before they had to sit in front of the assembled media pack and find the answers to what had only just happened.

After everyone had showered and changed clothes, the more senior players turned to the younger members of the squad and reminded them that they had just played in a World Cup final, in front of a world-record crowd, and they had finished an exhausting campaign. Soon the beers opened and the team livened up, but there were tears late into the night. Everyone felt flat. The team management had booked out a pub for them that evening, and family and friends were invited to join the celebrations for the tournament. It was bitter-sweet. Players were exhausted, sore and hugely disappointed. But they were also relieved. There is so much stress heading into a World Cup, and the pressure had built up exponentially as the team got closer to the final. It wasn't the perfect ending they had dreamed of, but for that night they enjoyed each other's company and reminisced about the tournament.

On the flight home, Emily couldn't sleep. She had so much nervous energy, sleep was the last thing she wanted to do. So she decided to watch the final. 'It's always so different to how you remember it and as I watched it I thought of *Bernard's Watch* [a kids' TV show in which Bernard could pause time]. If you had stopped the time as the ball was thrown in that final lineout, which had been our super strength, and asked who was going to win the World Cup, I think a lot of people would have said England,' Emily says.

When the team arrived home at Twickenham, there was another night out planned for them. The players enjoyed it so much it ended up being two nights out. Not only did they celebrate in the official afterparty, but they booked out the Cabbage Patch pub the next day and drank there too. Everyone got a plus one and Maud and Lucy Packer invited their mums. The two players were in bed by 9 p.m., but their mums carried on the party without them. The players knew these pubs had been booked before the World Cup, for celebrations, and instead there were only commiserations. How do you celebrate when you feel you have failed? 'People were congratulating us for coming second,' Emily recalls, 'and it felt so strange. I hated it, to be honest with you. We didn't feel like we had done enough for people to be patting us on the back and saying well done.'

Only a few days before the Red Roses' event in the Cabbage Patch, I had been hosting the final watch party at the same pub. On my post-match panel were two former England players, Ugo Monye and Giselle Mather. Tensions were high and it felt cruel to make a crowd, some of whom were in tears, listen to us talk about the match that had just ended. But what felt worse was making Giselle come on stage to speak about what felt like quite a personal tragedy. Giselle had coached many of these players and knew exactly how they would be feeling. 'The last thing anyone on that pitch needs right now,' Giselle said, pointing to the TV screens which I remember vividly showed Abbie crying, 'is me to criticise that performance. England gave everything, but sometimes in sport that's not enough.'

There was a sense on social media, for weeks after the final, that all criticism was unfair, and that the players needed protection from journalists who fairly called out the shortcomings of England's campaign. Ben Coles, the rugby reporter at the *Telegraph,* was sent nasty tweets because he had rated Lydia Thompson a four out of ten in his player ratings for the final. In the men's game, where journalists send in player ratings after every international match, such a rating would not raise any alarm. In fact a red card in a big match often gets lower than four in the men's game and Ben was being fairer than might have been expected. When New Zealand centre Sonny

Bill Williams was shown a red card during a Test match against the British & Irish Lions in 2017, the *Independent* rated him three out of ten, the *Guardian* gave him a two and the *Daily Mail* gave him a three.

I've never been a fan of player ratings. Journalists are often told to send them in at the final whistle, leaving little time to think about them, and they simplify performances in a mostly redundant way. The only person's opinion that matters to the players is their coach, but player ratings are for readers to debate and engage with. In the men's game, commenting on players' performances is the norm, yet with the Red Roses, fans often try to protect them and go after journalists who analyse their game in any way that isn't congratulatory and supportive. The players know when they haven't had a great game, and they don't need protection. They are athletes who understand the nuances of their individual game better than anyone sitting in the press box. But as the game grows, so will analysis and debate about players' performance, whether that is on social media or on the pages of broadsheet newspapers. The reaction from fans is mostly from a good place, of feeling protective of the supportive culture in women's rugby, but it is not productive in helping the game grow.

Of course journalism could be better, fairer and kinder, but journalists are not public relations employees of the RFU, and thank goodness they are not. It's not their job to build the confidence of players, but instead to accurately report on the sport and give well-reasoned opinions and analysis. Women's rugby must be taken seriously and treated with the same respect as men's. Journalists must be able to give fair criticism without petitions being drafted for them to lose their jobs, and fans should be free to share when they are unhappy with performances.

Off my soapbox and back to the panel. When we asked the crowd for questions, the first one was 'Surely Simon Middleton has to go now?' and some members of the crowd muttered in disagreement. A man in the crowd commented that Simon had just won 30 matches in a row, and it was just one loss, but a former Red Rose near the front said, 'He's had two chances to win the World Cup and he hasn't.' At that moment, it felt like eyes were darting around the room, unsure whether such a comment was fair or not. The truth was, nobody expected us to be having this discussion. As the presenter, I had a number of questions lined up for if England won, and only a few back-up questions for if they lost. The thought of Simon stepping down hadn't crossed my mind until that question. The panel, in the end, got their chance to give their opinions. Giselle gave a diplomatic but fair answer about the RFU needing to review the tournament, but Ugo was more cutting. 'He has to go,' he said. 'Midds is a great coach but when you have had two chances to win a World Cup and haven't, it's probably time for a change. He has to go.'

Chapter 7

THE ROAD TO REBUILDING

After the dust settled on the World Cup, the coaches reviewed the tournament. Louis Deacon felt the criticism of England's tactics were unfair, but he conceded that England didn't demonstrate to fans the full range of their abilities. 'We were winning and it was working,' he said. 'Why would you change something that's successful? On reflection, after the World Cup, we did have more in our game that we didn't use for one reason or another. We didn't deliver it consistently, playing the wider, more open game. We've done it, we've shown that we can do it in the past leading up to the World Cup. So looking back to some of the games, particularly the Canada semi-final and the final, there were opportunities that we didn't take that we should have.'

There was a period of mass change that followed the World Cup. The England squad regathered in February 2023 for a two-day debrief camp. Simon Middleton made clear it was not a training camp, so no need to pack your rugby boots, but it was a chance for the team to collect their thoughts about the tournament after the dust had settled. What had gone well? What were the team feeling ahead of a crucial Women's Six Nations campaign? Crucially, there would be no review of the final. The players had replayed the moments in their heads enough. The belief was nothing would be gained from going over old ground now.

In the camp were those who had played at the World Cup, some players who hadn't been selected, and some new players too. It was a 'mash-up of people in all kinds of different places', Emily Scarratt describes. 'I think for me, it probably came a bit late. There's no good time to do it though I guess, and I think we needed to do it at some point to draw a line under the World Cup and make sure everyone was on the same page for the Six Nations.'

On the first night of the debrief camp, the team all went out for a big team meal, taking over the whole top floor of a pub, and had food and a few drinks. There was a table plan to make sure players sat with people who weren't in their immediate friendship groups so that they could make stronger connections with those they hadn't spent much time with before.

For Simon, his feelings had been confused for some time. He always felt the same after major tournaments. There is a dip, when morale drops, and then there's a period of looking forward to the future when motivations are regenerated. Except this time, the wait for those feelings to regenerate was taking longer than he had expected. It suggested to him that he was ready for a new chapter.

The loss in the final had been a significant blow for the head coach. It was the second World Cup final he had lost with the Red Roses and the disappointment was taking a while to shift. Since landing home from New Zealand, Simon had regular calls with Conor O'Shea, the RFU's head of performance, to discuss the squad and how they could move forward. After weeks of conversations – each one including Conor asking, 'So, come on then, what do you think?' – Simon was nearing certainty on his decision about his own future.

Three months had passed since the Rugby World Cup final and the buzz had not yet returned. He knew his time with England was coming to an end. But first, he had to check in with the Thorns, to see if they were ready for a new voice to come into the camp. He could lean on the culture of honesty he had helped cultivate in the squad, and his senior team of players gave him an honest answer. Yes, they were ready for change too.

Emily Scarratt was having a coffee with some Loughborough Lightning team-mates when Simon called. 'When you see Midds' name flash up on your phone, you answer it,' she says. 'He said how we had been through a lot together so he wanted to let me know he was leaving.' Simon explained to her that he would be stepping down after the 2023 Six Nations.

'I speak really highly of Midds and everything he has done, but in this world you need fresh voices. You need new ideas and different ways of thinking about things or doing things. And I think that's really important. It's good to have something fresh, for us as a group, but also for them too, to have a new challenge and do something different.'

Simon was excited for the upcoming Six Nations, but the fire in his belly had quietened, and so came the realisation that it was time for a new voice in the camp.

Simon joined the RFU in 2014, initially in a role with England Sevens on the World Series, and took on the assistant coach role for the 2014 Rugby World Cup in

France, which England won. When Gary Street left the role in 2015, Simon became head coach of both the XVs side and the sevens team. He led the Team GB Women's sevens team to their fourth-place finish at the Rio 2016 Summer Olympics and upon his return his role focused exclusively on the XVs team.

During his tenure, he guided England to half a dozen Six Nations titles, including five Grand Slams, and a 30-match unbeaten run that set the world record in men's and women's rugby. He received personal recognition too and in 2021 became the first women's rugby coach to receive the World Rugby coach of the year award.

During the debrief camp, Simon took the Red Roses to Twickenham Stadium, to walk around the pitch. It was empty, cold and almost industrial-looking as maintenance work was under way to prepare for the men's Six Nations. They slowly walked around the pitch, reflecting on what the Rugby World Cup had meant to the team, to the players individually, to their families and to their fans.

They gathered in the middle of the pitch and spoke of the future, and how the players would feel on this very turf in 2025, when England host the Rugby World Cup. The final would be on this pitch and England should hope to have another chance of winning. They thought about how the sound system would be so loud they would feel the vibrations in their chest, how they would feel the warmth from the pyrotechnics next to the tunnel, how their hearts would be pumping so hard it would all feel like a dream. How the crowd would reach a crescendo as a player makes a break and runs for the line. Hearing 'try for England' before their name is called out to a packed stadium. Seeing family and friends in the crowd – maybe even lifting the World Cup in front of them.

Individually, each player thought about it, some knowing they too would be a face in the crowd. Captain Sarah Hunter was one of them. She decided during the 2021 Rugby World Cup that she would be in the stands by the time 2025 came around, but even in the week leading up to the semi-final she had no thoughts on when that retirement would come. 'I want to sit in the crowd, watching England play and feeling proud of how I helped them get there,' she said that week, 'but I have no plans for my retirement yet.'

Simon directed the team into the changing rooms, which had just been renovated to reflect the achievements of the Red Roses. Despite Twickenham being the national stadium for both the men's and women's teams, for a long time it had felt like playing in the men's stadium. The first time the Red Roses played a stand-alone fixture there would come in that Six Nations tournament, in 2023 against France, and it attracted a world-record crowd of 58,498. The changing rooms had been built for men but were slowly modernising to be more comfortable for the women – including small touches like a sanitary bin in the toilets. Their achievements, Women's Six Nations Grand Slams and the 2014 World Cup, adorned the walls, finally. This was their space too now. The team sat around the changing room, with Simon in the middle, similar to how it would be on a game day, and he told the team he would not be there in 2025. The team needed a new voice, he explained to them, someone with new vision. Eyes darted around the room, trying to capture the reactions from team-mates. Simon thought some faces looked happy, some looked shocked, some were sad. Everyone was silent.

The players' views on Simon are mixed. Some wished he had chatted to them more or found him cold, some found that they clashed in personality, but all respected him. 'Midds is a classic Yorkshire bloke,' Emily says. 'He has a really good heart and he doesn't take any shit from anyone. He's pretty forthright with what he thinks but he has always wanted the best for us.'

Simon's time with England will be remembered for the record-breaking 30-match unbeaten run England enjoyed under his leadership. What the coach will remember with regret are the moments of defeat, including the 2021 World Cup final. It was the second successive World Cup final that England had lost under his leadership. It was not the way Simon wanted to finish things with England, but he was certain that the time had come for someone else to take over.

So what was his legacy? In his own view it is the role he has played in accelerating the growth of women's rugby in England, adapting the style of rugby the Red Roses play that changed the face of international rugby, and the part he has played in creating a robust programme of women's rugby in England.

'People talk quite a bit about legacy and what that means, and I think it means different things to different people,' Simon says. 'To me I think going from about 3,000 fans at games to over 58,000 for England vs France in the 2023 Women's Six Nations is a legacy. I'm hugely proud of the growth that the team have managed to create. To have it reflected on an occasion like that [England vs France game] was an amazing point to be able to step away. So I think that the growth of the game is a huge part that I certainly stop and reflect really positively on.'

Aside from the off-pitch growth, Simon is proud of how he has developed women's rugby not just in England but across the world. 'The quality of play we've been able to develop across the game of rugby and particularly helping that tactical understanding of various ways to play, is something I'm very proud of,' Simon reflects, a month after he 'hung up his whistle' for England.

'If you look at the lineout, for instance, or the kicking game, where it was to where it is now, it's a different world to when I started coaching England. You look at how England are now, with one of the best lineout technicians in the world in Louis Deacon. And we have some of the best lineout technicians in the world in Abbie Ward and Zoe Aldcroft. So I'm hugely proud of growing that side of it, and just the whole size of the programme, the infrastructure, and the Premier 15s [now the Premiership Women's Rugby] league.'

Winning became Simon's 'obsession', because he recognised the symbiotic relationship between the on-pitch success of the Red Roses and the speed of change within the sport. The team's accomplishments have driven growth and amplified support from influential figures within the rugby community. The allure of the Red Roses, both on and off the field, has attracted sponsors and stakeholders who are eager to associate themselves with the team's success, and fans of all ages gather for selfies with the players.

Simon saw his role in helping women's rugby as making England the most successful team so that the money would follow.

'Because of the success we had, people want to be associated with the Red Roses, they want to come to our games, and they want to speak to the players,' he says. 'So that's another part and ultimately, at the top of my agenda has always been winning because I know that winning drives change, and if you want to be successful as a coach or a player you've got to win. Really, winning has become an obsession over the last couple of years. I've been obsessed with finding ways to keep winning.'

Scott Bemand, the team's attack coach, decided he would also leave his role, and in July 2023 he became the Ireland Women's head coach. Louis Deacon would stay.

Shortly after Simon announced he would step away from England, captain Sarah Hunter announced her retirement, but not before England played Scotland at Kingston Park in her home town of Newcastle. 'I've waited too long for the Red Roses to go to Newcastle; I'm not missing it,' she said with a grin on the build-up to the 2023 Six Nations. Sarah had begun playing rugby on the fields in the shadow of Kingston Park stadium but her final dance would be under the spotlight. The build-up to the match was 80 per cent about Sarah Hunter and 20 per cent about the match. There was no mistaking that this was Sarah's match, and everyone else was just an accessory. As the woman of the hour, it was fitting that her farewell would be on the hour mark of the match. Sarah was substituted off and every player on the pitch, including Scotland, stopped to give her a round of applause. The stadium was on its feet and no try got a bigger roar that day than Sarah's farewell. With teary eyes and her trademark grin, the international hero left the pitch and England Rugby's greatest servant closed the curtains on her career.

'Not many athletes get to choose how and when they call

time on their playing careers,' Sarah said after the match. 'I'm very fortunate that I have the opportunity to finish on my own terms. I couldn't think of a better way to do it than in my home town, where my rugby journey started.

'I get to finish in a place that has a special place in my heart in front of my friends, family and Red Roses supporters and I feel very fortunate that I'm able to do that.

'To play there in a white shirt – which is something I've been immensely proud of and I feel very honoured to have represented my country so many times – feels like an ending I couldn't look past and I feel very fortunate that I get to do this.'

Sarah's departure was the first domino to fall, as both Simon and Scott would remain in post until after the Six Nations. Marlie stepped up to the captaincy role, which she has taken to marvellously, and has led the team with her unmistakable brand of passion. Simon and Scott's final game in charge was England's Grand Slam victory against France in that year's Six Nations, in front of a world-record crowd. A wonderful way to end their tenures.

In May 2023 it was announced that John Mitchell, the former All Blacks head coach, would be taking over from Simon. Louis Deacon remained in post, and Lou Meadows, the under-20s head coach, moved into the attack coach role. Sarah Hunter also took up her new post as transition coach. Emily Scarratt had been asked to be on the panel involved in the interview process, but the timings didn't fit in with her busy schedule as she recovered from an ankle injury. There was a senior Red Roses player on the interview panel, yet the identity of the new coach was not shared between the players, many of whom had their own theories of who might be their new coach as they relaxed in a 2023 Six Nations camp. A couple of players had heard the new coach was a woman, and I was interrogated by Poppy Cleall, who recited names of prospective coaches to me to see if she could infer anything from my reactions. It was quite the interruption to an interview about nutrition, but it was nice to see that Poppy has a good future as a detective.

The team eventually found out via Twitter, thanks to a journalist breaking the story before the RFU had spoken to the players. 'Literally the following day, Charlie Hayter arranged a call with me, him, Marlie and John, and then a few days later we had a whole team call to confirm and let everyone know the rest of the coaching set-up,' Emily said. But Marlie was on holiday when the meeting invite landed in her inbox, so Emily had to text her: 'You might want to jump on the call with the new head coach.' Marlie quickly joined the call.

John has been a controversial figure in rugby union. He is a decorated coach who joined England with almost three decades of international coaching experience with New Zealand, Australia, South Africa, USA, Japan and England. He was part of the England men's set-up as a forwards coach between 1997 and 2000 and defence coach between 2018 and 2021.

There was speculation on social media that his coarse attitude might disrupt the culture of the Red Roses, which had taken years to rebuild. Fans suggested that because John had not coached women before, he might be too harsh on the players, with some fans also worrying that players would not be able to stand up for themselves against him. Those comments made Sadia Kabeya, the England flanker, chuckle. 'We are strong women,' she says, laughing when recalling the comments she had read on social media. 'We have always stuck up for ourselves, and the older players especially will have no problem saying something if it doesn't work out. We trust that he is the best man for the job, but I guarantee that if any issues arise, the players will be the first to call it out.'

Louis Deacon stepped up as interim head coach before John, who was contracted with the Japan's men's team until the end of the 2023 World Cup in the autumn, started the role. Louis was excited to work with the seasoned recruit. 'I've got a lot to learn from him,' he says. 'The coaching staff now is fairly young and a bit less experienced so having a heavyweight like John is the right approach I think.'

Under new leadership, the team could then look ahead to the future. But as we begin to look at what the future holds for this Red Roses team, it's important to consider the roadblocks that lie in their path off the pitch. Rugby union is a tough sport, for men and women, and the challenges along the way cannot be underestimated.

Chapter 8

ROADBLOCKS TO SUCCESS

Rugby union is facing a crisis. The number of brain injuries, including concussion, are rising and the evidence of its link to dementia and other neurodegenerative brain diseases is strengthening. Hundreds of former players, including at least six women, have taken legal action against World Rugby, England Rugby and the Welsh Rugby Union accusing the governing bodies of negligence in their failure to protect them from brain injuries during their careers.

Steve Thompson, the 2003 Rugby World Cup winner with England, was diagnosed with early onset dementia when he was 42 years old. He was one of the first eight former players to launch the legal action and all were under the age of 45. All eight received the same diagnosis: early onset dementia with probable chronic traumatic encephalopathy (CTE), for which the only known cause is repeated blows to the head. CTE is diagnosed as probable because it can only be diagnosed for certain in a post-mortem dissection of the brain. That group of eight was just the start. Soon hundreds of former players, mostly in their forties and fifties, got in touch with Richard Boardman, the lawyer representing the players at Rylands Law, to say they had similar symptoms.

Steve was capped 73 times for England and three times for the British & Irish Lions, yet he barely remembers anything, especially not winning the World Cup. 'You see us lifting the World Cup and I can see me there jumping around. But I can't remember it,' he told the *Guardian* shortly after his dementia diagnosis. 'I'd rather have just a normal life. I'm just normal. Some people go for the big lights, whereas I never wanted that. Would I do it again? No, I wouldn't. I can't remember it. I've got no feelings about it.'

The first sign for Steve that something was wrong happened when he was living in Dubai. He left a work meeting and realised he couldn't remember anything that was said. Soon, his family noticed too and his young children would remind him that he had promised to do a chore around the house, or that he was wrong when he told his wife that she hadn't asked him to do something. Because of his memory issues, his performance at work was affected and soon the family had to leave Dubai. Then one day Alix Popham, a former Welsh rugby player who had been diagnosed with early onset dementia, called Steve and told him of his own symptoms – memory loss, emotional distress, feeling withdrawn – and Steve said, 'Shit, you're explaining me, here.' Alix suggested Steve get tested and the results were worse than feared.

His memory was assessed by seeing if he could recall a list of 20 words, and he could only remember five. It was at that moment he realised he was in trouble. Steph, Steve's wife, had lost her nana to dementia the year before and she said to the specialist doctor that it was as if her husband had dementia, but she also did not believe he could be affected in his forties.

Brain scans showed extensive damage to his brain, which a consultant told him was similar to the impact of a fatal car crash. Instead of one big crash, the damage had been formed, Steve says, by the repeated blows to the head that happen while playing rugby. Those repeated blows caused sub-concussive injuries, which have caused damage over time as parts of his brain have slowly died.

There have been moments when Steve cannot remember Steph's name, and his children can now recognise the facial expression he makes when his mind has gone blank on their names too. He has come close to suicide, including going to a train station with the intention of jumping in front of a train. Life is difficult, but he is now learning to live with dementia. His consultant told him his brain is like an old Nokia phone battery; it still works, but it needs recharging a lot more regularly. So that's what he does. He has a routine, has got back into fitness again, and he tries to rest as much as he can. He knows of former players who have ended their own lives and he sees players further down the road than he is.

Rugby was never Steve's big love, despite him being at the top of the game. The accolades are so meaningless to him that he only found his World Cup medal – rusty in the bottom of a bag – when he was asked to find it by a documentary crew. 'People say, "Would you do it again?", and personally I wouldn't,' he says. 'I wouldn't be where I am now if I had the choice.'

Rugby union is not alone. Boxing, American football, football and a number of contact sports are facing the same challenge. How do you contend sport's entertainment factor and the desire to play, with the undeniable fact that there is a link between repeated head impacts, brain injury and dementia?

In 2022, concussion rates in elite rugby hit the highest levels since records began, and the first multiple season study of injuries in elite women's rugby in England found that concussion was the most common specific injury diagnosis.

But most of the research available focuses on men and boys. Worryingly for the women's game, there is growing evidence that concussion and brain injury affects women and girls differently to men and boys, with some research suggesting the link between concussion and dementia is stronger in female athletes than male athletes.

Tracey Covassin, a prominent researcher into concussion in sport, found that female sportspeople are twice as likely to suffer concussions as males playing the same sport, and her research also found that males and females are likely to report different symptoms in the following days and weeks.

For example, while men are more likely to report amnesia, women are more likely to report prolonged headaches, mental fatigue and mood changes. The research also found that female athletes need more recovery time than men before they are symptom-free. One study of 266 teenagers – including footballers, American football players, wrestlers and skiers – found that women took an average of 76 days to recover, while men took 50 days.

Women are more susceptible to concussion for a number of reasons. On a biological level, neck strength is a key reason why women and girls sustain more concussions. Concussions are caused by a sudden movement in the brain which damages the brain cells and causes them to release chemicals which alter how the brain works. They are often the result of the head moving or stopping suddenly, such as when the head hits the ground, or moves suddenly in a whiplash motion. The head is supported by the muscles in the neck and men tend to have a lot more soft tissue around their necks than women. You can check this for yourself easily by seeing if you can join your two hands around your neck. Women tend to be able to do this easily, whereas men find it harder because their necks are bigger.

This means men have a greater ability to control their heads in contact and especially when falling. Dr Elisabeth Williams from Swansea University researched the comparative neck strength in the university sides at Swansea University – a high-performance rugby environment – and found that even the weakest male player's neck strength was significantly higher than the strongest neck strength in the women's game. This means men are significantly better prepared to prevent concussions happening compared to women, as they have greater control of their heads.

The Red Roses have been training for neck strength since 2014 and neck strength is a key part of the Red Roses' training plans. They have also used in-game technology to track the number and severity of their impacts, as well as making sure players are not doing too much contact training. At the 2021 Rugby World Cup, all players were offered smart mouth guards, by Prevent Biometrics, which were able to track collisions in live time for the frequency and magnitude of head contact and head accelerations.

In addition to neck strength, hormonal variations also play a role in the increased susceptibility of women to concussions. Research has shown that hormonal fluctuations throughout the menstrual cycle, particularly the decline in oestrogen levels just before the period, have been linked with increased concussion symptoms and longer recovery time. Furthermore, some research suggests that women taking oral contraceptives may have a higher risk of concussion due to the synthetic hormones in the pill. Oral contraceptives can alter hormone levels in the body, which can potentially affect brain function and increase the likelihood of sustaining a concussion. This research is at an early stage, but underlines the importance of considering factors unique to women in sport, particularly considering that most concussion research is conducted on men.

There is also the argument that women and girls are more susceptible to concussion because of the age they begin playing rugby. Women and girls tend to start playing rugby later than men and boys, due to factors of accessibility and interest. Especially in the elite game, men tend to have begun playing rugby union at a minis or junior level, meaning they are taught tackle technique from a younger age and have more experience of playing rugby by the time they progress to senior rugby. In theory, their rugby skills are therefore more advanced. Many women do not begin playing rugby until they are 18, and therefore do not have the same exposure to rugby as men have at the same age. It's important to note that while women may be more susceptible to concussions, factors like good technique, experience and neck strength can help protect women.

Concussions also affect women differently to men. Women can experience different symptoms, mechanisms of injury and recovery time. When it comes to symptoms, research suggests that women may experience certain concussion-related symptoms more frequently or with greater intensity than men. While there are common symptoms shared by both sexes, such as headaches, dizziness and difficulty concentrating, women may also be more likely to report symptoms like fatigue, depression and sleep disturbances.

In terms of how concussions are sustained, women and men may report differences in the mechanisms of injury. Research suggests that women may be more susceptible to concussions resulting from contact with an opponent's body rather than head-to-head collisions. Women also tend to have a higher incidence of concussions resulting from accidental clashes during tackles or falls, indicating a potential difference in tackling technique.

The final difference in how men and women present with concussion is the recovery time. This can vary but studies suggest that women take longer to recover than men. This could be partly due to various factors, including hormonal influences, as fluctuations in oestrogen levels throughout the menstrual cycle can impact recovery.

While research is developing, practical interventions like the head injury assessment (HIA) being rolled out in the women's game is a positive step towards helping medical professionals and coaches identify concussions and limit the risk of subsequent head clashes, which can prove incredibly dangerous.

For Kat Merchant, who was part of the Red Roses team who won the Rugby World Cup in 2014, the impact of concussion forced her to retire before the rest of her body was ready. 'I had 14 recorded concussions, and I've been knocked out at least five times,' she recalls. 'And I think if I was playing nowadays, I'd have been made to retire a lot earlier than I did. With the last concussion I had, I had a seizure on the pitch and it was really scary for everybody else. Everyone around me sort of looked at me differently and questioned whether I should be playing. We were a year out of the [2014] World Cup, so of course I'm going to play. So I came back and played, but I just never was the same from that point. I didn't think about anything else, I guess, because I had just signed a professional sevens contract, which was super exciting.

'The [2014] World Cup final for me was really emotional for two reasons. One, we had won the World Cup and it was amazing, but also I knew it was the last time I was ever going to play rugby. I knew there was no way because during that World Cup, even someone brushing past me in a ruck was enough for me to see stars and feel dizzy and I was getting symptoms from smaller and smaller things. So there is no way I can play professional rugby week in, week out and knock my head. It's just not a position I can put myself in. So I put it aside, played the World Cup, and then buried my head in the sand a little bit about it for a few weeks afterwards, just enjoying what was happening. Then I spoke to a neuroscientist and they were like, "It's probably time to retire; I would if I was you." They can't tell you what to do, but they made it clear that it was time.'

Kat has signed up to a programme with the Rugby Players' Association that arranged lots of tests on her brain to understand if the concussions had left lasting damage. 'Since I retired they have brought out a better MRI that can tell us more about the brain so I had that done, and I had loads of tests done, including memory stuff. It's quite funny, because they give you ten words to remember and then say them back. I said to them, "I've got to warn you now, I remember those words from nine years ago when I was playing." They give standard words like apple and bubble, and I did them so often that they're still in my memory now, so they had to use different ones.

'Luckily for me my brain looked good, everything was clear and the structure of my brain was fine. I think what saved me was because I was an amateur, those concussions were spaced out and I didn't have contact every day.'

Maud Muir has also suffered with concussion and similarly felt that her brain had become more susceptible to smaller knocks since being concussed. Maud sustained her first in training before the 2021 Six Nations and then had a second in her first game for her club after the tournament. She missed all games of the Six Nations. 'My eyes felt weird, I couldn't describe it,' Maud says. 'I saw an optician, a dentist, and I even got Botox in my temples. They actually put it down to stress in the end, like tension headaches, but I do sometimes get headaches here,' she says, gesturing to her temples. 'I think it was definitely caused by the concussion. I know that for a fact. But it was all just a bit of a blur because I was so focused on trying to get back for the [2021] World Cup. It was obviously a very stressful period and I had a few dark days where I wasn't sure if I wanted to do rugby. I just didn't want to have a headache any more.'

Players are supported by England Rugby with mandatory rest periods, and staff care deeply about the risk of concussion and support further research into that area of science. The Rugby Players' Association (RPA) refers former players to the Advanced Brain Health Clinic, which is run by the Institute of Sport, Exercise and Health, to help them find out more about their brains and support them if there is damage which raises concerns about their brain health. There is also a 24/7 confidential counselling service for players, funded by the RPA's charity Restart, which can support players who have been seen by the Advanced Brain Health Clinic.

Concussion is a heavy topic for rugby players. It's the silent threat in the back of their minds as they try to focus on their short careers. But it must be addressed and greater research is paramount to make sure that women are as safe in the sport as possible. As women become more ingrained in rugby union, the sport must recognise the differences in women's bodies and make sure women are able to make informed choices about the sport.

Rugby must also acknowledge that there are new challenges that only the women will face. Pregnancy is a peculiar challenge for women's rugby players. In the UK, employees have to tell their employer they are pregnant at least 15 weeks before the beginning of the week the baby is due, but World Rugby say no pregnant woman should play rugby, due to the obvious danger to both the mother and unborn child in the highly physical sport. When you play rugby at an elite level and are on a professional contract for your club or country, those working rights are effectively thrown into question. Once the pregnancy is known about, the player has a duty to inform their coaches. Essentially, players are forced to reveal their pregnancy earlier than traditional workers, which some players say makes them concerned about the future of their employment.

In non-contact sports there are mothers who have excelled while pregnant or after giving birth. Tennis legend Serena Williams won the Australian Open, one of tennis's major tournaments, while eight weeks pregnant, athletics star Jessica Ennis-Hill won a World Championships gold medal and an Olympic silver medal after giving birth, and Laura Kenny, the record-breaking Team GB cyclist, won a gold and silver medal at the 2020 Olympic Games after giving birth in 2017.

But when your job involves people tackling you at speed, being lifted in lineouts or scrummaging, many women decide to wait until they retire from rugby union to start a family, and risk waiting until their retirement age, often late thirties, to begin the process of trying to conceive.

For one player, who does not wish to be named, her plan had always been to retire from rugby and then try to conceive a child. She had watched other players do that, and had only given a small amount of thought to whether she would be able to conceive. In her mind she was a fit and healthy woman who had eaten well and kept a healthy lifestyle, so she believed she would be able to conceive naturally fairly quickly.

Having seen former team-mates retire and seemingly have no issues conceiving, her own fertility was almost an afterthought to her. But after a year of trying, she went to a private clinic and faced doctors questioning her suitability for IVF due to her age. She was in her early forties.

For the former Red Rose, she had not even considered having children while playing at the highest level of rugby. She had watched team-mates retire when they became pregnant, wished them well, but was so comfortable with her choice to focus on rugby – something she still does not regret at all – that there was no jealousy or desire to join them on the touchlines with babies strapped to their chests.

Having children was always part of her plan, part of her partner's plan too, but as she settled into retirement she soon realised that they might have left it too late to conceive naturally. The player is still weighing up her options after two unsuccessful rounds of IVF.

Marlie Packer became a mother in 2020 to her son Oliver. The flanker feels lucky that Oliver's other mum was the one to carry him, so the pregnancy had a minimal effect on her rugby career. She recognises that rugby careers are short and players want to make the most of the small amount of time spent at the top of the game.

When Oliver was born, in the midst of the Covid-19 pandemic, Marlie did not need to go on parental leave because there was no training or matches to be missed and her body was unaffected by his arrival, apart from the lack of sleep. Her position is fairly unique in the women's game.

When the players received their full-time professional contracts in 2019, the maternity policy was standardised with the policy that RFU office workers receive. The contracts were the first of their kind, revolutionary in their field – but this was a hurdle still left to climb.

Players such as Vickii Cornborough worked with the RPA to drive change. As part of a three-year process to form the new policy, the RFU, alongside the RPA, looked at those on offer to sportswomen around the world. New Zealand Rugby introduced a tailored maternity policy in 2018, but the Welsh Rugby Union, who introduced professional contracts in 2022, did not have a tailored policy in place for players when they turned professional.

In football, women's players in the WSL and Championship reached an agreement in 2022 for 14 weeks of maternity leave on full pay, significantly less than is now on offer by the RFU.

In February 2023, the RFU announced a new maternity, pregnant parent and adoption policy for the Red Roses. It acknowledged the many different types of parenthood the players experience, and supported them throughout the pregnancy or adoption and for one year after the child is introduced to the family. It gives the players 26 weeks' maternity leave on full pay, plus enhanced job security when they are pregnant. If at any point during pregnancy or while on maternity leave their contracts are renegotiated or extended, the player will have their contract extended for a minimum of 12 months.

The policy also covers practical support for childcare after birth, to help the mother return to work. Any player who returns from maternity leave within 12 months of giving birth or adopting a child can bring them, plus a support person, who is expected to assist in the care of the child, to training camps and matches. The RFU covers all travel and accommodation costs for the support person and the child.

Once the player informs the RFU of their pregnancy, they will be offered a full risk assessment to understand which duties can safely be performed during their pregnancy. Players can shadow the training sessions and learn more about coaching while it is safe for them to do so, or can coach rugby in the community.

England Rugby will also pay for pregnant players to have prenatal and postnatal checks by specialist physiotherapists, to help them through the process of pregnancy, giving birth and then returning to play rugby.

The first two players to take advantage of the deal were Abbie Ward and Vickii. In January 2023, Abbie announced that she was expecting her first child with husband Dave, who himself is an ex-England and Harlequins rugby player. She gave birth to her daughter Hallie on 20 July 2023, only two days before Vickii gave birth to twins Elizabeth and Charlotte.

Returning to international rugby after giving birth is still a rare occurrence. Abbie was the first player to do so in England colours since Emma Croker in 2012. However, there is some precedent in England for players continuing to train while pregnant. Allianz Premiership Women's Rugby player Davinia Catlin was taking part in sessions with Harlequins Women until she was 28 weeks pregnant, while being heavily monitored by doctors and coaches, and returned to rugby when her son Caden was only 12 weeks old, playing her first game postpartum in September 2021 while still exclusively breastfeeding. It's becoming more common, too, and Deborah Wills played a full 80 minutes for Worcester Warriors only 17 weeks after giving birth.

The maternity policy was an important step in the right direction and players are regularly pushing for better terms in their contracts. As chapter two touched on, in the past there has been a divide between players and the RFU about what the contracts should look like and how much the players should be paid. 'I think we see how undervalued women's rugby is so as players we want to have our say as much as possible,' Maud says. 'We really do put our bodies on the line and put in so many hours, and only now in the last couple of years are people starting to be rewarded for it. I think the higher powers think: "We're giving them something so they should be grateful." But everyone [all the players] says no, we need to push for more. We can't just settle with having contracts, they need to be good contracts that actually value us.'

There will undoubtedly be learning curves as the policy is put into action with different players and different types of parenthood, but the important thing is that all sides keep an open mind to how women can raise children while playing rugby.

There are other issues that will only affect women too – including better understanding how the menstrual cycle affects performance, or why women's sports stars are so susceptible to ligament injuries – and rugby must continue to invest in valuable research in those areas.

It all forms part of rugby union getting used to women being a crucial part of the game. The other side to that is the players becoming accustomed to the outside pressures of being in the public eye. As women's rugby develops, so does the media coverage and social media commentary about the game. For the most part it's wonderful and there has been a relative boom in high-quality coverage since 2020. In 2019, I published my Master's degree dissertation on the UK media coverage of women's rugby, and can see a drastic improvement from my findings then. I considered Premier 15s (now Premiership Women's Rugby) match attendances, volume of social media interaction with women's rugby content, and readership figures of women's rugby pieces in national newspapers to find that there was significant interest that was not being met with enough coverage.

I also reviewed all published women's rugby and men's rugby stories across the BBC, the *Telegraph*, the *Daily Mail*, the *Guardian* and *The Times* in a two-week period and found that there were more mistakes in the women's rugby coverage than men's, such as spelling names wrong or misidentifying players in photos. It should be noted that Scrum Queens, the dedicated women's rugby website, was by far the best source of accurate and considered women's rugby news and analysis – and I would argue that the website remains the best source on both current and historical women's rugby news. I concluded that there was sufficient interest and knowledge for more coverage of a higher quality.

Since then, women's rugby content is far more common in most national papers. The *Guardian* and the *Telegraph* lead the way with live blogs during games and the latter's women's sport section, now led by former *Rugby World* editor Sarah Mockford, is an excellent source for stories about the off-pitch issues in women's rugby such as the ones discussed in this chapter. There are also now social media content creators whose careers are focused solely on creating women's rugby content, a good sign that there is clear demand for coverage. And on a personal note, I've noticed first-hand how the comment sections on my articles have moved on from 'nobody cares', to more thoughtful and knowledgeable debate about players or tactics. There are still one or two comments from the 'nobody cares' brigade but those are now interspersed with fans who love the game and want to engage with the content.

If it wasn't for journalists publicising what women's rugby players around the world earn, the Red Roses would not have been able to use those figures in their own contract negotiations and therefore secure a pay rise. Journalists in England have written extensively about the challenges the

England team face and have given a platform to players to speak up about issues. But in recent years, journalists are increasingly being confronted by directors of rugby, coaches and even players, accused of not helping to grow the game when they report on players not performing well or predict a team will lose. Women's rugby needs great public relations people, skilful content creators and brilliant press officers. It also needs hard-working journalists. Women's rugby is too good for the media to patronise fans by pretending it's perfect all the time.

We are in a transition period as coverage moves away from congratulating England for doing so well with little resource, to expecting the highest standards of the best-supported team in the world. While the players in general enjoy greater coverage, their higher profile comes with increased scrutiny. Not all of it is good, and to this day some rugby journalists (who almost exclusively cover men's rugby) are allowed to write bizarre pieces with out-of-date information that criticise the women as if they entered the professional game from the same academy structures and access to rugby from a young age as the men's players did. They compare Zoe Harrison to Owen Farrell, as if he didn't have exposure to elite rugby from birth thanks to his rugby league star of a dad, Andy Farrell.

Kat is now a pundit in the media and has to find the balance between being able to critique players while also shedding light on the reality of life as a women's rugby player, which she knows well. 'As a pundit, you've got to be critical because you've got to expect a good standard, otherwise you're assuming it isn't a good standard. But you've also got to humanise players. I got very protective of Lydia

[Thompson] during the [2021] World Cup because she was tagged in things online that were awful. One person tagged me and her in a tweet that said she got her red card on purpose. Who gets a red card on purpose? She's a lovely, lovely person and I hated how people were talking about her. She actually came off social media completely because of it.

'Social media is a whole other thing. A lot of the men [England's men's team] have people controlling their social media accounts so they don't tend to see what people are saying about them,' Kat explains. 'But the women will have these notifications pop up on their phone when they're doing something normal like having a cup of coffee with their mum, and it can be really hurtful.'

The pressure and scrutiny the players are under makes their jobs a different challenge to the women who came before them. Whereas Kat's struggles in her career were battling a lack of resources for the women's game and managing working on top of playing for England, the team were generally praised in the media for their sacrifices. Now, the current crop of Roses have a lot of support but have the new challenge of trying to manage the higher standards they are held to.

'When we lost [the] 2010 [Rugby World Cup], there was little media coverage and what did get through was always like, "Wow they're great, they're amateurs doing this alongside their jobs and they're amazing." Whereas now, there's been that transition to, "Well, they're paid. They're professionals and they need to have the same critique that the men have." Now I'm not saying they should get the same critique, but the more support you get the more backlash you get if you don't reach those standards. When they lost [the 2021 World Cup], there were a lot of people saying it's not good enough. Now, working in the media, I go to Premiership Women's Rugby games where there are 4,000 fans and England have 50,000 fans and as a player I definitely would have enjoyed that pressure, but I chat to my friends who still play and they say how hard it can be.

'The huge new fan base is really cool but it comes with more pressure; there is a lot of pressure,' Kat says. 'And if someone has a bad game, and that's all over the internet, that can be quite tough. I remember just at the end of my career newspapers had just started rating us and a teammate got a five or a four, and it was brutal. If I had got one of those I would be gutted. That new side to it can be quite stressful.'

There are a number of incredible players who have become pundits in the women's game: Mo Hunt and Emily Scarratt both have a fantastic way of going deep into the detail of play without overloading viewers with information, and the supremely talented Kat brings life and energy to all games. Simon remarks that so many players with sound rugby minds – Emily and Mo are two examples he uses – go into punditry when they are injured, because they are so tactically astute that broadcasters love having them on air talking about rugby. He wonders whether there will be any former players left for coaching if they all go into punditry.

'We've got to make coaching appealing to players in terms of careers, because I think it's appealing to them in terms of the idea of staying in the game that way, and they enjoy working with other players, but ultimately, I'm pretty sure they enjoy punditry too,' he says. Simon names Mo and Emily, as well as Abbie, as players he thinks could make top-level coaches in the women's game, thanks to their rugby brains and years of experience at the highest level.

'We're in competition against punditry and I'm not quite sure if people see the danger in it,' Simon says. 'But I think there's a huge danger that we could lose this crop of potential coaches to punditry. I don't think you can do both. Now the game continues to grow to the highest level, I don't think you can do both. Not to the extreme that some of them have been doing. And, you know, Scaz [Emily] has done lots while she has been injured, but you can't do that amount of punditry if you want to be a head coach, or if you want to be a full-time coach.'

There are many more incredibly talented former players who are now pundits, and at risk of forgetting someone, special mention should go to Nolli Waterman, Maggie Alphonsi, Rachael Burford and Katy Daley-McLean. They have all helped fans get closer to the game with excellent reporting. Their role is a tough one: by their very nature they want to grow the game but they also must show that they're not so biased they can't be critical.

As the players become more well known, another challenge has been facing creepy comments from people, mostly men, online. It's an updated version of the oversexualisation of women rugby players that has happened since its infancy. In chapter one, Gill Burns detailed the time she had to wear a tutu for a newspaper photoshoot. In Gill's house she has scrapbooks full of newspaper clippings from her career. As she flicks through the pages, she reflects that players saw it as their duty to go ahead with these features. They thought that distasteful coverage was better than no coverage and at least it made people aware that women play rugby. There were a few journalists who covered the sport in all its glory in the 1980s and '90s, but the majority of coverage could be summarised as: 'Cor! Look at these women. They're trying to play rugby, and look – this one is pretty!'

In years gone by, women's rugby players have been asked to wear high heels with their kit for photos and asked questions about their sexuality in interviews. Today's players have the protection of press managers and, hopefully, editors who realise that the least interesting thing about women's rugby players is how they look.

Kat remembers being sexually harassed while playing for England in 2010: 'We were playing at Twickenham and there weren't many fans around. There was a man who shouted, "Oi, number eleven, great arse." Unfortunately I think it's something that's always going to exist in one way or another. It's a societal thing, not a rugby thing, and it's only going to stop when people in their friendship groups are able to call them out on it.'

Comments on social media still remain an issue for current England players, and Jess Breach has had men make sexually suggestive comments about her on her Instagram page. 'You want to post photos when you're on holiday, maybe a bikini picture, but you know you're going to get sexual or rude comments that you're not going to appreciate,' Jess said on the *O2 Inside Line* podcast. 'It gets you down and I think for me personally, I've had a couple where they're not that bad – like "your arse looks good" – but why have you done that? Do you want me to slide into your DMs and say, "Oh, thanks!" If I was walking down the street and some-one wolf-whistles or says, "You've got a banging body,", that is sexual harassment. But if someone comments that on a picture on a social media platform, nothing [happens]. I should feel safe posting on social media and know that I'm not going to get hate or abuse from it.'

The final part of this book will look ahead to the future. No player I have ever met is more astute to the need for retirement plans than Jess Breach. She has explored brand and commercial deals as a player, has a degree in sports marketing and communications and is keeping her mind open to the opportunities that might present themselves upon retirement.

Not all players are as prepared for life after rugby as Jess, and the RPA have been working with the Red Roses through its personal development programme, called Gain Line, to help players prepare for life after rugby. The representative body was appointed as the exclusive welfare representatives for the squad in August 2021, and the squad has a dedicated player development manager as part of the Gain Line programme, Lynsey Hyslop, who regularly helps players find new opportunities, including career days for the Red Roses with the BBC and Sky Sports, as well as trade skills taster sessions at a college.

Rugby is a short career but the benefit the women's team has is that for many of them, they didn't grow up planning to be professional players, so they were able to make sure they didn't have all their eggs in one basket. Men's players, on the other hand, often find themselves stuck after retirement, facing a drop in earnings and less concrete plans for the next step in their journeys. That is a whole other issue, but one that, thankfully, women's rugby is yet to truly face.

Women's rugby is not perfect. It faces the challenges that men's rugby does too and the rising number of brain injuries, including concussion, in rugby union is a concerning crisis that cannot be ignored. There are also key debates and issues that affect the women only, which must not be sidelined in rugby's future. The Red Roses are real women who face the issues that life throws to us all, with concerns for their futures, aware that rugby does not last forever, so they continue to push for more.

Chapter 9

BUILDING A LEGACY

The Red Roses now face their most formidable challenge yet: hosting the World Cup in 2025. The pressure is on England to right the wrongs of the last tournament. The weight of expectation and potential rests on their shoulders.

So how do they go one step further and lift the World Cup in 2025, in front of a Twickenham Stadium crowd? 'When John Mitchell joined he spoke of needing to turn winners into champions, and I think he is exactly right,' Louis Deacon says. 'It's really just those things that can make a 1 per cent or 2 per cent difference now. You look at how we lost the World Cup final [in 2022] and the game can all come down to one lineout, one throw, one chance to score. So now the focus of our training will be about being 1 per cent better and becoming champions, not just winners.'

The challenge on the pitch will be to go one step better than before without becoming entangled in trivial details while searching for those 1 per cent improvements. Off the pitch, the 2025 World Cup presents a unique opportunity for England to capture the spirit of the nation.

The RFU set ambitious objectives for the tournament in

2022, having been selected as hosts, with a headline target of selling out Twickenham for the final – a final England fervently aspire to be playing in. A test run during the 2023 Six Nations decider between England and France demonstrated the women's game's commercial potential. It was supposed to be an examination of how close the RFU were to being able to sell out Twickenham, with RFU data suggesting they would sell under 30,000 tickets. The reality was almost double that: a world-record crowd for a women's rugby match with 58,498 fans in attendance.

The atmosphere was joyous. The crowd roared for every move of the ball, not just the tries. Good passes were being applauded, the crowd shouted 'Oooo' in unison every time a big hit went in. They were entirely engaged with the play on the pitch. In men's rugby, the complaint during every Six Nations tournament is that there are fans in the stadium who are drunk and aggressive, or make you move so they can get to the bar during the play. At Twickenham on that day, there were groups in fancy dress enjoying their beer and singing loudly, but there was not that feeling that there could be a fight at any moment.

The significance of that match extended beyond demonstrating the magnitude of the women's rugby fan base. It illustrated the distinctiveness and progressiveness of that fan base too. The attendees comprised families enjoying a relatively affordable day out and groups of young people having a great time. The question of whether all the spectators were diehard rugby fans or simply there for the experience becomes inconsequential. The enjoyment of the game does not require a minimum level of understanding. Rugby should shed its elitist image and embrace inclusivity.

Rather than pricing out families, the men's game should learn from the women's game. The vibrant and engaged crowd at Twickenham that day exemplified the potential for a more accessible and welcoming rugby culture. The half-time performance from the Sugababes was good too.

In the crowd was Gill Burns, the former England rugby player, who sat with a group of former Red Roses and their families. Before the match, they had been in the room for the England Rugby Internationals Club (ERIC). It was the first time that former Red Roses had been invited into the room, which is usually only occupied by men. It was agreed that on that day, the room should be full of former Red Roses and that efforts should be made to include women in ERIC. Membership, which costs £10 a year, ensures the former players have somewhere to sit and have a quiet drink and a bite to eat before and after games in the stadium. There are now ongoing talks between ERIC (which is a separate body to the RFU) to include women in the membership.

Gill was surrounded by the mates she had played with for England and she stood with tears in her eyes as the players, including two players she had coached, ran out of the tunnel. Gill had taken Holly Aitchison and Sarah Beckett to Twickenham before when she had coached them at school. Now they were running out to sing the national anthem in England's first ever stand-alone women's fixture at the national stadium. 'I was just blown away,' Gill says. 'You're standing amongst great friends whom you've had fantastic rugby journeys with. And just none of us said anything. I looked around and everyone had glassy eyes, but we were just speechless.'

Over an hour after the final whistle, the stadium was still at least a third full as fans waited to get selfies and autographs from their favourite players. If the Red Roses could find a way to sign 58,498 signatures, they would do so. After every match they stay way past what would be considered the polite medium and interact with as many fans as they possibly can, because they know how important their role is in carrying the rose forward and inspiring the next generation of Red Roses.

After the match the funfair in the car park was in full swing, with children running around in England shirts revelling in the atmosphere. There were women's rugby teams in their club shirts and some in fancy dress. I was pleased that I had not been sitting behind the ten women dressed as bananas who I saw trying to win a huge fluffy octopus from one of the stalls.

The Red Roses have played around the country in recent years, including Doncaster, Exeter and Newcastle, in a bid to grow the fan base around the country. That day at Twickenham felt like all of those fans coming together to show just how big the fan base is.

While all eyes are on the Rugby World Cup final at Twickenham, which should break that world record, the tournament will not only take place in London. The Red Roses will play in different regions across the country to attract as many fans as possible, rather than playing all matches in London or the surrounding areas. It will generate interest around the country and hopefully make sure that the stadium is sold out for the final.

In 2010, when England last hosted the tournament, all matches apart from the semi-finals and the final were played in Surrey, with the finals played just up the road at the Twickenham Stoop. Public interest was higher than the tournament organisers anticipated, with the final drawing in a crowd of 13,253 – a world record for attendance at a women's rugby international match at the time. The 2,500-capacity Surrey Sports Park sold out for the first two days of pool-stage matches, as was the third day despite the organisers increasing the capacity to 3,200. A considerable fan base was there, 15 years before England host their next tournament, but they were not given the same opportunities. The growth of women's rugby since then means the 2025 tournament offers a real chance for further expansion in England.

For Sue Day, the former Red Rose who is now the RFU's chief operating officer and chief finance officer, hosting the tournament offers the chance to emulate the success of other England women's sports teams who have hosted World Cups, including cricket, netball and hockey. She believes it will advance all women's sport, not just rugby, and encourage women to try something new.

Rugby has the chance to follow in the success of the Lionesses, the England women's football team, who truly captured the nation's attention when they lifted the European Championship trophy in 2022 and came so close to claiming the World Cup the following year.

UEFA and the FA released a flash impact report following the Euros, measuring the immediate impact of the tournament. 'Unprecedented' was a word too many of us became bored of in 2020, thanks to the coronavirus pandemic, but there is no better way to describe a tournament which for the first time kept newspapers full of women's sport, radio shows abuzz with chats about manager Sarina Wiegman's selection decisions, and punters as keen to throw their pints in the air when England score as they were when the men's England team reached the Euros final in 2021.

Unprecedented. Unrivalled. Oversubscribed. The tournament was hosted across ten venues in England, with the final taking place at a sold-out Wembley Stadium. Getting tickets was difficult. Even some of the England men were denied tickets due to the sheer demand, and it was clear that Harry Kane and Co. had only really started paying attention to the women's game once it was popular.

The flash impact report, produced by Ernst and Young, found that the total match attendance for the tournament was 574,875, including 110,555 international spectators who travelled to the UK from 104 countries. The average attendance for each match was 18,544 and the final was attended by 87,192 fans – the record for a European Championships final, in the men's or women's game. According to the report, 85 per cent of those who attended are likely to attend professional women's football events in the future (88 per cent would watch a match on TV), and 84 per cent of spectators said the tournament improved their perception of women's football.

There was a 289 per cent increase in the media rights values since the previous women's Euros and it was the most watched women's Euros ever, with a global live viewership of 365 million, across 195 territories.

Then there is the media coverage. Let us start with the traditional print media which, unfortunately for people like me who love it, is dwindling in readership. Women's sport remains underserved in most newspapers – the *Telegraph* and the *Guardian* being the current exceptions to that. But it is exactly where we should look if we want to understand how significant the change was.

Sports editors tend to significantly favour men's sport. That's not because the editors are nearly always men – there are plenty of men in these roles who enjoy women's sport. It's mostly because they are battling for every inch of space in the newspaper, and women's sport is usually not read as much as men's sport, so it's an easy thing to cut.

I know from personal experience working with national newspapers and smaller publications that to get a women's sport story in print, it has to be something big and often stories that are huge in the sport are given little coverage because the latest Premier League transfer rumour has bumped it out of the edition. The women's Rugby League World Cup, hosted in England in 2022, passed by with little mention in the national press, outside of the BBC and the *Telegraph*.

But on the day after the Euros final nearly every national newspaper's front or back page had Chloe Kelly, the England goalscorer, running triumphantly with her shirt off. It's important to consider print, because the readership tends to be over-fifties, more male than female, with less interest in women's sport than those who get their news online. Yet editors recognised that this sporting event had truly captured the attention of people from all generations in England. Not all people loved it, there were people still desperate to compare it negatively to the men's game, and there are people who don't like football, regardless of the gender playing it. But enough people were interested for all sports editors to recognise its value. That is one of the biggest signs of success in the coverage of women's football, even if print readership is less than one third of the total readership of newspapers. Most people read on their phones, tablets or computers.

There has always been something special about a print newspaper too. It's a record of what happened on that day and the cut-throat nature of what gets in the paper means only the top stories are included. It's a dwindling readership but it's marvellous to pick up a warm newspaper and read the stories and solve the puzzles without being asked if you accept cookies and battle through a million different pop-ups with impossibly small Xs to close them. The importance of print might be dying, but the recent boom in women's sport coverage at national newspapers is truly something to be noted. It suggests genuine interest, not token coverage, of women's sport.

So from the old age of print newspapers, let's turn to the most modern, terrifying prospect for journalism: social media. Globally, the Euros generated 453 million social media interactions, with TikTok (39 per cent) and Twitter (21 per cent) contributing the most towards that number.

There was a good economic boost, too. According to UEFA and the FA, host cities received an £81 million increase in economic activity as a result of the tournament. That was made from domestic and international visitors who made over 552,000 day and overnight trips to host cities and includes the £44 million in total spectator spending around matches and trips across England.

There are sponsors who truly value women's rugby and whose support means they have become an integral part of its growth. O_2, front of shirt sponsor and principal partner of England Rugby, signed a landmark five-year deal in 2020 to become the first sponsor to equally fund the men and women's teams. As part of that sponsorship they co-funded the *Wear the Rose: An England Rugby Dream* documentary about the Red Roses, which aired on ITV two days ahead of the Rugby World Cup and was watched by over 1.25 million people. Research from The Women's Sport Trust found that those who watched the documentary consumed an average of 68 minutes of action during the Rugby World Cup on linear TV, compared to 44 minutes for those who didn't.

Their focus now is on continuing to close rugby's gender awareness gap and the 'Journey to 82', which is O_2 and the RFU's shared mission to fill the 82,000 seats at Twickenham Stadium for a Red Roses match. Part of that journey is making the match-day experience more inviting and fun for women's rugby fans.

The effect of England hosting the Euros in 2021 was enormous. Unprecedented, even. Can rugby achieve anything close to that when the nation hosts the World Cup in 2025?

The journey of the England women's rugby team has been one of resilience, determination and progress. From battling against historical gender stereotypes to carving out a place in a traditionally male-dominated sport, these women have defied expectations and shattered barriers. Their story is one of inspiration and empowerment, resonating far beyond the realm of rugby.

The Red Roses have not always triumphed on the pitch, but they have become ambassadors for change, promoting inclusivity and diversity in a sport that has often been perceived as exclusive and elitist. They have shown that rugby is not just a game, but a catalyst for social progress and empowerment.

These chapters have not been a pat on the back for a team who know themselves they haven't achieved what they are capable of. But they have been a tribute to their perseverance, camaraderie and spirit in the face of adversity. The next step for the team to take together is one of strong communication and building on the foundations of their success.

As you close this book, I want you to think back to chapter one, of the women's rugby match stopped by a man horrified by what he saw. Next, think of that first World Cup in 1991, the world governing body uninterested in the tournament and fans few and far between. Now imagine the 2025 World Cup final, which should hopefully sell out Twickenham Stadium. Think of the colours, the sounds and the smells as that stadium fills with over 80,000 women's rugby fans. The women who will walk down the tunnel and enter the noise of that stadium will be standing on the shoulders of all the women who came before them, and once more, they will raise the bar for the girls in the crowd who will become Red Roses in their future. And while there is so much to celebrate, the same battles that women faced at the inception of the sport are still there today. There are still men who think women shouldn't play rugby, and while the Red Roses are mightily supported, they also have new fights on their hands; for commercial interest, player wellbeing and so much more. The issues might now be different, or developed, but they are still there.

As the players sit down to reflect on their achievements and their losses, they look ahead to their own futures. Their thoughts all turn to the Rugby World Cup.

'I want to run out with Oliver as my mascot at the 2025 World Cup final,' Marlie says.

Maud would be happiest if she is a core member of England's starting XV by the time the World Cup rolls around, Emily just wants to still be playing. 'It's my intention to train and work towards playing in the 2025 World Cup, but I don't know what my body will allow,' she says. Upon her retirement, Emily is undecided over whether she will head into coaching, punditry or neither. Jess is clear: she wants to win the World Cup, and she's not really fussed on how the team get there.

'I want my daughter to be sitting in the crowd, seeing me in an England shirt, with "Ward" on the back and a winner's medal around my neck,' Abbie says.

But that's all for the next, yet unwritten, chapter. And how marvellous that will be.

Bibliography

Chapter 1: The pioneers

Birch, J., 'Remembering WRWC '91: The Soviet Union', Scrum Queens, 2016. Available at: https://www.scrum queens.com/features/remembering-wrwc-91-soviet-union

Buckley, W., 'The forgotten story of . . . the Dick, Kerr's ladies football team', the *Guardian*, 2009. Available at: https://www. theguardian.com/football/blog/2009/sep/09/england-women-football

Furse, L., 'Cardiff v Newport: The Ladies' Story', World Rugby Museum, 2018. Available at: https://worldrugbymus eum.com/from-the-vaults/womens-rugby/cardiff-v-new port-the-ladies-story

Gillibrand, P., 'Armistice Day: WWI Wales Women's Radical Rugby Movement', BBC News, 2022. Available at: https://www.bbc.co.uk/news/uk-wales-63584615

Hands, D., 'American brawn to advantage', *The Times*, 1991

Joncheray, H., *Women in Rugby* (London: Routledge, 2021)

Ruskin, J., *Sesame and Lilies* (London: Yale University Press, 2002)

'Women's Rugby, A Brief History with Dr Lydia Furse', YouTube, 2021. Available at: https://www.youtube.com/watch?v=uGvPqbrJguc

Chapter 2: Growing Roses

Slot, O., '"Will it take a strike to resolve this?" – Women's rugby contract crisis', *The Times*, 2018. Available at: https://www.thetimes.co.uk/article/will-it-take-a-strike-to-resolve-this-womens-rugby-contract-crisis-fm28rbz6s

'Women's Rugby World Cup: Ireland Stun New Zealand', BBC Sport, 2014. Available at: https://www.bbc.co.uk/sport/rugby-union/28637552

Chapter 3: It takes a certain kind of woman

Lowe, A., 'Use women's law changes as blueprint to rewrite rules of rugby, says Wasps Ladies coach Giselle Mather', *The Times*, 25 March 2021

Tomas, F., 'Maud Muir can become England's most destructive front-row operator', *Daily Telegraph*, 19 November 2021

Vernon, P., 'Bradley Wiggins: the coach who abused me – and why I hated cycling', *The Times*, 5 May 2023. Available at: https://www.thetimes.co.uk/article/bradley-wiggins-cycling-coach-abuse-olympics-tour-de-france-8m9lndwgn

World Rugby, 'Learning from her father's mistakes; Marlie Packer on parenting | The Open Side', YouTube, 1 July 2021. Available at: https://www.youtube.com/watch?v=d-iIHwc3-rY

Chapter 4: A holistic vision of success

The Well HQ, 2023. Available at: https://www.thewell-hq.com/

Chapter 5: More than a maul

Westerby, J., 'Women's Six Nations: Louis Deacon's long journey from Moseley's lineout to world No 1s', *The Times*, 2022. Available at https://www.thetimes.co.uk/article/womens-six-nations-louis-deacons-long-journey-from-moseleys-lineout-to-world-no1s-67b3j0t9k

Chapter 6: 2021 Rugby World Cup

Henson, M., 'Women's Six Nations: Natasha Hunt on England return', BBC Sport, 2022. Available at: https://www.bbc.co.uk/sport/rugby-union/60839526 (Accessed: 29 June 2023)

Hunt, M., 'New faces, big debriefs: The World Cup catch up,' The Good, The Scaz and The Rugby, YouTube, 2021. Available at: https://www.youtube.com/watch?v=oC1mv9GVn18

Kitson, R., England overpower Australia in rain-soaked

Rugby World Cup quarter-final, the *Guardian*, 2022. Available at: https://www.theguardian.com/sport/2022/oct/30/england-reign-supreme-in-stormy-41-5-quarter-final-defeat-of-australia-at-rugby-world-cup (Accessed: 29 June 2023)

Chapter 8: Roadblocks to success

Aylwin, M. and Bull, A., 'Rugby World Cup winner Steve Thompson reveals he has dementia and joins landmark legal case', the *Guardian*, 2020. Available at: https://www.theguardian.com/sport/2020/dec/08/steve-thompson-former-rugby-union-players-dementia-landmark-legal-case

Breach, J., *England Rugby O2 Inside Line* podcast, 11 October 2022

Meagher, G., 'Concussion rates in elite rugby hit highest levels since records began', the *Guardian*, 21 June 2022. Available at: https://www.theguardian.com/sport/2022/jun/21/concussion-rates-in-elite-rugby-hit-highest-levels-since-records-began

Starling L.T., Gabb N., Williams S. et al., 'Longitudinal study of six seasons of match injuries in elite female rugby union', *British Journal of Sports Medicine* 57, February 2023, pp. 212–17

Chapter 9: Building a legacy

England Rugby, 'England to host Rugby World Cup 2025', 2022. Available at: https://www.englandrugby.com/news/

article/england-to-host-rugby-world-cup-2025 (Accessed: 31 January 2023)

UEFA.com, 'UEFA Women's Euro 2022 positive impact and future legacy revealed in post-tournament', Flash report: Inside UEFA, UEFA.com, 2022. Available at: https://www.uefa.com/insideuefa/news/027a-164415be92b2-36f88ae7c9ec-1000–uefa-women-s-euro-2022-positive-impact-and-future-legacy-reveal/ (Accessed: 19 January 2023)